Quick Reference Guide™

Quicken® 4

for Windows™

Berkemeyer/Chassman/Kuhr

14 East 38 St New York, NY 10016

First Dictation Disc Printing

10 9 8 7 6 5 4 3 2

Catalog No. G7

ISBN: 1-56243-242-7

Printed in the United States of America

INTRODUCTION

The **DDC**® **Quick Reference Guide for Quicken**® **4 for Windows**™ will save you hours of searching through technical manuals for keystrokes and/or mouse actions.

Quicken 4 for Windows tasks may be accessed in several ways:

- Using the mouse from the main menu.
- Using keystrokes from the main menu.
- Using the mouse to access commands from the icon bar.

Tasks are listed alphabetically, and the template featured on the back cover provides a fast reference to Quicken 4 for Windows special keys and window movement commands.

Before You Begin...

You should become familiar with **INTRODUCTORY BASICS**, page ix, which includes illustrations and descriptions of Quicken 4 for Windows screens and terminology.

Quicken is a "user–friendly" program with a great deal of "built–in redundancy". This means most commands can be accessed in a variety of ways. In most cases, however, we have chosen to show you only one or two ways to do a task. If you follow the procedures step–by–step, you will be able to perform any task you desire. As you become more comfortable with Quicken, though, you may want to play around with the program and discover other ways to complete the same tasks. In most cases, there is no right or wrong way. It's all personal preference.

Authors:	**Joseph M. Kuhr**
	Milton Chassman
	Kathy Berkemeyer
Technical Editors:	**Bill Moy**
	Kathy Berkemeyer
Managing Editor:	**Kathy Berkemeyer**
Director of Publications:	**Don Gosselin**
English Editor:	**Rebecca Fiala**
Layout:	**Kathy Berkemeyer**
	Rebecca Fiala

Special thanks to Will Weisman of Intuit for providing software and technical support.

ii

TABLE OF CONTENTS

TABLE OF CONTENTS (continued)

TABLE OF CONTENTS (continued)

TABLE OF CONTENTS (continued)

TABLE OF CONTENTS (continued)

vii

viii

TABLE OF CONTENTS (continued)

INTRODUCTORY BASICS

Quicken 4 for Windows Desktop Window

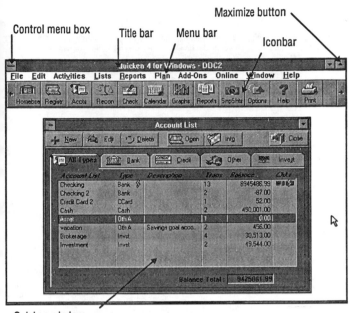

Maximize button

Control menu box · Title bar · Menu bar · Iconbar

Quicken window

Quicken 4 for Windows Desktop Parts Descriptions:

• Control menu ⊟	Clicking once opens menu; clicking twice exits Quicken 4 for Windows.
• **Title bar**	Displays program title.
• **Maximize** ▲	Clicking once expands window to a full screen. After window is maximized, the Maximize button is replaced with Restore button *(see page xv)*.
• **Menu bar**	Displays main selections from which pull–down menus may be accessed.
• **Iconbar**	Contains buttons representing commonly used menu items.
• **Quicken window**	Displays the current account or activity. More than one Quicken Window can be open at a time.

Quicken Window

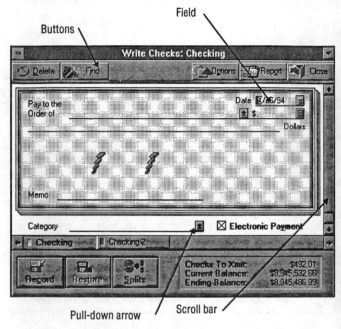

Field

Buttons

Pull-down arrow

Scroll bar

Quicken Window Parts Descriptions:

• **Field**	Click and enter data (e.g. Address).
• **Scroll bars**	Click these arrows to view other parts of worksheet.
• 🔽	Click to display pull–down menu.
• **Buttons**	Click to take desired action.
• 🔽	Click to minimize current active Window.

Homebase

Provides another way to access some of Quicken's most frequently used features.

To display Homebase:

a. Click  Homebse .... |Alt| + |H|

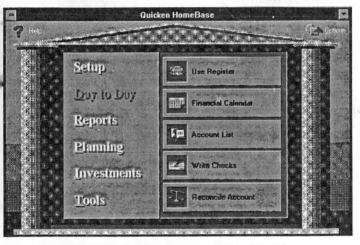

THE **QUICKEN HOMEBASE** SCREEN APPEARS.

b. Click desired Section:

- | **Setup** | .... |Alt| + |S|

- | **Day to Day** | .... |Alt| + |D|

- | **Reports** | .... |Alt| + |R|

- | **Planning** | .... |Alt| + |P|

- | **Investments** | .... |Alt| + |I|

- | **Tools** | .... |Alt| + |T|

Click desired button

To change Homebase options:

Click desired options.

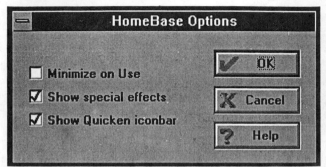

ACCESS COMMANDS

Use Menu Bar

1. Use the mouse to point to a menu bar item.
2. Click once.

   OR

   Use the keyboard to access a menu bar item (press **Alt** + the underlined *letter* on menu item).

   Note the main menu bar:

| File | Edit | Activities | Lists | Reports | Plan | Add-Ons | Online | Window | Help |

A **pull–down menu** appears listing commands:

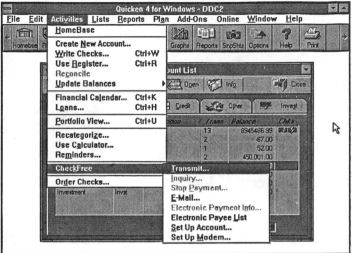

Pull–down menu items with an **arrowhead** means a
cascade menu follows. A cascade menu is a submenu of
the selection.

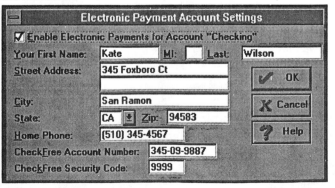

Pull–down menu items with an **ellipsis** (...) following the
word indicate another window or a **dialog box** follows. A
dialog box asks for additional information to complete a
task.

xiv

MANAGE WINDOWS

Activate Window

Click anywhere in desired window.

OR

a. Click <u>W</u>indow menu............................ **Alt** + **W**

The title of the active window will be checked.

b. Click window title.................. **↑** **↓** **→** **←** , **↵**
    you want to activate.

Open Control Menu

1. Click **Control** box ▣........................... **Alt** + **-**
    of desired window (located in the top left corner of
    any window).

2. Click desired item .... **↑** **↓** , **↵**

*There are two types of windows: **application** and **document**.*
Quicken *4 for Windows screens are displayed as document
windows.*

Maximize Window

Click **Maximize** button ▲
of desired window (located in top right corner of
specified window).

OR

a. Click **Control** box ▣........................... **Alt** + **-**

b. Click Ma<u>x</u>imize.. **X**

> *NOTE: The **Restore** button (see below) replaces
> the **Maximize** button after window is
> maximized.*

Restore Window

Click **Restore** button ⬍ of desired window

OR

a.   Click **Control** box ⬜ .... `Alt` + `-`

b.   Click **Restore** .... `R`

Minimize Window

Click **Minimize** button ▾ of desired window
(located in top right corner of the specified window).

OR

a.   Click **Control** box ⬜ .... `Alt` + `-`

b.   Click **Minimize** .... `N`

Restore Minimized Window

Double–click window icon you want to restore.

OR

a.   Click **Control** box ⬜ .... `Alt` + `-`

b.   Click **Restore** .... `R`

Close Window

Double–click **Control menu** box ⬜.

OR

Press **Ctrl+F4** .... `Ctrl` + `F4`
to close window.

OR

1.   Click **Control** box ⬜ .... `Alt` + `⬜`

2.   Click **Close** .... `C`

ACCOUNTS

Set Up New Account

1. Click **Accts**

*The **Account List** appears.*

Account List tabs

Account List buttons

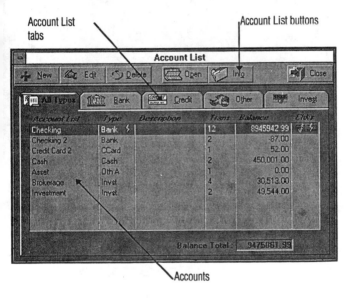

Accounts

2. Click **＋ New** .... Alt + V, N

*The **Create New Account** dialog box appears (see page 2).*

continued...

Set Up New Account (continued)

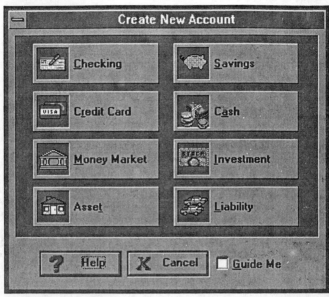

*NOTES: If you want Quicken to guide you through setting up a new account, select **Guide Me** and complete steps a-d, below.*

*If you do **not** want to be guided through set up, complete steps 3-4.*

—WITH GUIDE ME SELECTED—

a. Choose one of the following account types:

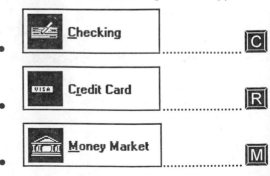

continu

Set Up New Account (continued)

- **Asset** .... T

- **Savings** .... S

- **Cash** .... A

- **Investment** I

- **Liability** L

b. Enter required information.

c. Click **>> Next** .... Alt + X

d. Click **✔ Done** .... Alt + D

— *WITH GUIDE ME DESELECTED*—

3. Choose one of the following account types:

- **Checking** C

- **Credit Card** .... R

- **Money Market** .... M

continued...

4

Set Up New Account (continued)

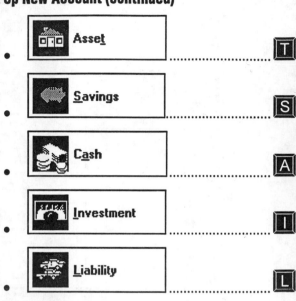

- **Asse**t .... T
- **S**avings .... S
- **C**ash .... A
- **I**nvestment I
- **L**iability L

4. Enter the appropriate information for the type of account selected.

   NOTE: The type of information required in this dialog box depends on the type of account selected.

Checking

1. Select **A**ccount Name .... Alt + A
2. Type name .... *name*
3. Select **B**alance .... Alt + B
4. Enter amount .... *amount*
5. Select a**s** of .... Alt + S
6. Change date .... *date*
   if necessary.

contin

Set Up New Account—Checking (continued)

If account is tax–deferred (earnings are not taxable until you collect them)**:**

Click **Tax–Deferred Account** .... `Alt` + `T`
–IRA, 401(k),etc.

To enter optional Information:

a.   Select **Description** .... `Alt` + `D`

b.   Type description .... *description*

c.   Click .... `Alt` + `I`
     and enter desired information.
     *(See **ADDITIONAL ACCOUNT INFORMATION**,
     page 13.)*

d.   Click [✔ **OK**] .... `↵`
     to return to **Account List** window.

Credit Card Account Without IntelliCharge

1.   Select **Account Name** .... `Alt` + `A`

2.   Type name.. *name*

3.   Select **Balance** .... `Alt` + `B`

4.   Enter amount...*amount*

5.   Select **as of** .... `Alt` + `S`

6.   Change date .... *date*
     if necessary.

*(See Setup New Account: Credit Card Account with
Intellicharge, page 6, if you plan to use this as an
IntelliCharge account.)*

continued..

6

Set Up New Account—Credit Card Account Without IntelliCharge (continued)

7. Deselect **Enable IntelliCharge** if it is selected.

   To enter optional information:

   a. Select **Description** .... Alt + D

   b. Type description .... *description*

   c. Click [📁 Info] .... Alt + I
      and enter desired information.
      (See ADDITIONAL ACCOUNT INFORMATION, page 13.)

   d. Click [✔ OK] .... ↵
      to return to **Account List** window.

Credit Card Account With IntelliCharge

1. Select **Account Name** .... Alt + A

2. Type name .... *name*

3. Select **Balance** .... Alt + B

4. Enter amount .... *amount*

5. Select **as of** .... Alt + S

6. Change date .... *date*
   if necessary.

7. Select **Enable IntelliCharge** .... Alt + N

continu

Set Up New Account—Credit Card Account With IntelliCharge (continued)

8. Click **Credit Card Number** .... Alt + C

9. Enter valid credit card number .... *number*

   NOTE: *See Quicken documentation for applying for valid card through Intuit.*

10. Click **Credit Limit** .... Alt + L

11. Enter limit .... *amount*

12. Click >> More... .... Alt + M

13. Enter required information.

14. Click ✔ **Done** .... Alt + D
    when finished.

continued...

Set Up New Account (continued)

Money Market Account

1. Select **Account Name** .... `Alt` + `A`

2. Type name .... *name*

3. Select **Balance** .... `Alt` + `B`

4. Enter amount .... *amount*

5. Select **as of** .... `Alt` + `S`

6. Change date .... *date*
   if necessary.

   If account is tax–deferred (earnings are not
   taxable until you collect them)**:**

   Click **Tax–Deferred Account–IRA,** .... `Alt` + `T`
   401(k),etc.

   To enter optional information:

   a. Select **Description** .... `Alt` + `D`

   b. Type description .... *description*

   c. Click [📁 Info] .... `Alt` + `I`
      and enter desired information.
      *(See ADDITIONAL ACCOUNT INFORMATION,
      page 13.)*

   d. Click [✔ OK] .... `⏎`
      to return to **Account List** window.

continu

Set Up New Account (continued)

Asset Account

1. Select **A**ccount Name .... `Alt` + `A`

2. Type name .... *name*

3. Select **B**alance .... `Alt` + `B`

4. Enter amount .... *amount*

5. Select a**s** of .... `Alt` + `S`

6. Change date .... *date*
   if necessary.

   If account is tax–deferred (earnings are not taxable until you collect them):

   Click **T**ax–Deferred Account–IRA, ... `Alt` + `T`
   401(k),etc.

   To enter optional information:

   a. Click **D**escription .... `Alt` + `D`

   b. Type description .... *description*

   c. Click [📁 Inf**o**] .... `Alt` + `I`
      and enter desired information.
      *(See **ADDITIONAL ACCOUNT INFORMATION**, page 13.)*

   d. Click [✔ OK] .... `↵`
      to return to **Account List** window.

continued...

Set Up New Account (continued)

Savings Account

1. Select **Account Name** .... `Alt` + `A`

2. Type name .... *name*

3. Select **Balance** .... `Alt` + `B`

4. Enter amount .... *amount*

5. Select **as of** .... `Alt` + `S`

6. Change date .... *date*
   if necessary.

   If account is tax–deferred (earnings are not
   taxable until you collect them)**:**

   Click **Tax–Deferred Account–IRA,** .... `Alt` + `T`
   401(k),etc.

   To enter optional information:

   a. Select **Description** .... `Alt` + `D`

   b. Type description .... *description*

   c. Click 🗁 Info .... `Alt` + `I`
      and enter desired information.
      *(See **ADDITIONAL ACCOUNT INFORMATION**,
      page 13.)*

   d. Click ✔ OK .... `↵`
      to return to **Account List** window.

continu▶

Cash Account

1. Select <u>A</u>ccount Name .... Alt + A

2. Type name .... *name*

3. Select <u>B</u>alance .... Alt + B

4. Enter amount .... *amount*

5. Select a<u>s</u> of .... Alt + S

6. Change date .... *date*
   if necessary.

   If account is tax–deferred (earnings are not
   taxable until you collect them)**:**

   Click <u>T</u>ax–Deferred Account–IRA, ... Alt + T
   401(k),ctc.

   To enter optional information:

   a. Select <u>D</u>escription .... Alt + D

   b. Type description .... *description*

   c. Click [📁 Inf<u>o</u>] .... Alt + I
      and enter desired information.
      *(See **ADDITIONAL ACCOUNT INFORMATION**,
      page 13.)*

   d. Click [✔ OK] .... ⏎
      to return to **Account List** window.

continued...

Set Up New Account (continued)

Investment Account

1. Select **A**ccount Name .... **Alt** + **A**

2. Type name .... *name*

3. Select **B**alance................................... **Alt** + **B**

4. Enter amount ....*amount*

5. Select a**s** of................................... **Alt** + **S**

6. Change date....................................*date*
   if necessary.

   If account contains a single mutual fund:

   Click **Account contains a** .... **Alt** + **M**
   Single Mutual Fund.

   If account is tax–deferred (earnings are not
   taxable until you collect them)**:**

   Click **T**ax–Deferred Account–IRA, ... **Alt** + **T**
   401(k),etc.

   To enter optional information:

   a. Click **D**escription................................ **Alt** + **D**

   b. Type description........................... *description*

   c. Click ⌕ Info .... **Alt** + **I**
      and enter desired information.
      *(See **ADDITIONAL ACCOUNT INFORMATION**,
      page 13.)*

   d. Click ✔ OK .... ⏎
      to return to **Account List** window.

ADDITIONAL ACCOUNT INFORMATION

Records detailed information about selected account. You can record this information as you are creating a new account, or you can add it after the account is already created.

—FROM ACCOUNT LIST WINDOW—

1. Select desired account .... [↓] [↑]

2. Click [📁 Info] .... [Alt] + [O]

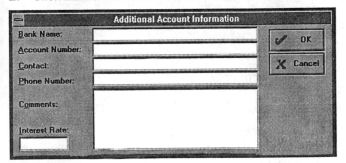

3. Enter desired information:
   - Bank Name
   - Account Number
   - Contact
   - Phone Number
   - Comments
   - Interest Rate

4. Click  OK .... [↵]

Edit Account

—FROM ACCOUNT LIST WINDOW—

1. Click account to edit.

2. Click [🏠 Edit] .... `Alt` + `I`

3. Make necessary changes to account information.

4. Click [✔ OK] .... `⏎`

    NOTE: *If you are editing a Credit Card Account,*
    you will be asked to enter the new credit
    card limit.

Delete Account

—FROM ACCOUNT LIST WINDOW—

1. Click account to delete.

2. Click [🚫 Delete] .... `Alt` + `D`

3. Type *yes* .... `Y` `E` `S`

4. Click [✔ OK] .... `⏎`

Create Savings Goal Account

Allows you to set aside money from a regular Asset Account toward a savings goal.

This money can be made available to the Asset Account again by transferring the money back from the Savings Goal Account.

1. Click **Plan** .... Alt + A

2. Click **Savings Goal** .... Alt + S

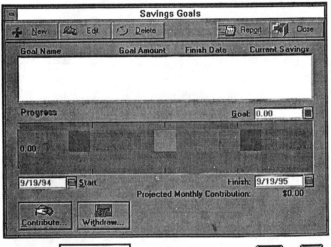

3. Click ✚ **New** .... Alt + N

Create Savings Goal Account (continued)

4. Enter savings goal information:

   - <u>Go</u>al Name

   EXAMPLE: Vacation, Car, New home, etc.

   - Goal <u>A</u>mount
   - <u>F</u>inish Date

5. Click [✔ OK] .... [↵]

Quicken calculates the monthly contribution.

Contribute to Saving Goal

1 Click **Pl<u>a</u>n** .... [Alt] + [A]

2. Click **<u>S</u>avings Goals** .... [S]

3. Select desired goal .... [↓] [↑]

4. Click [Contribute...] .... [Alt] + [C]

5. Click **<u>F</u>rom Account** .... [Alt] + [F]

6. Select desired account .... [↓] [↑]
   from which to contribute.

continu

Contribute to Savings Goal (continued)

7. Click [✔ OK] ....[↵]

8. Click [⬛ Close]

Spend Money in Savings Goal Account

To spend the money in a Savings Goal Account, you must transfer the money back into your checking account.

1. Click **Plan** .... [Alt] + [A]

2. Click **Savings Goals** .... [Alt] + [S]

3. Select desired savings goal .... [↓][↑]

4. Click [Withdraw...] .... [Alt] + [T]

5. Click **Put funds back in** .... [Alt] + [P]

6. Select desired destination and amount.

7. Click [✔ OK] ....[↵]

    *NOTE: When the Savings Goal Account has served its purpose, delete it. Quicken removes all transfers involving the Savings Goal Account from the checking account registers. The checking account **Ending Balance** box now displays the true balance.*

ACCOUNT BALANCES REPORT

1. Click Reports

2. Click **Other**.. **Alt** + **E**

3. Click **Account Balances**.................. **Tab**, **↓** **↑**

4. Click **Customize** .... **Alt** + **C**

5. Select desired report dates from **Report Dates** list.

   OR

   a. Click **from** box .... **Alt** + **F**
      and enter date.

   b. Click **to** box.................................. **Alt** + **O**
      and enter date.

   *NOTE: At the **from** and **to** boxes, you can also*
   access the drop–down calendar from
   which you can select starting and ending
   dates.

6. Click **Title** box.................................... **Alt** + **I**

7. Type report title ....*title*

8. Click **Interval** box .... **Alt** + **V**

9. Select desired interval for column headings from
   list.

10. Click **Organization** box .... **Alt** + **Z**

11. Select desired options.

continu

ACCOUNT BALANCES REPORT (continued)

If you want amounts rounded to nearest dollar:

Deselect **Cents in Amounts** .... `Alt` + `S`

12. Click **Accounts** .... `Alt` + `A`
    in **Customize** box.

13. Select each account to include in report from
    Accounts Used box.

    OR

    Click `Mark All` .... `Alt` + `M`

    OR

    Click one of the following **Accounts Used** buttons
    to select all accounts in that category:

    - `Bank` .... `Alt` + `B`
    - `Cash` .... `Alt` + `H`
    - `Credit Card` .... `Alt` + `D`
    - `Investment` .... `Alt` + `I`
    - `Asset` .... `Alt` + `S`
    - `Liability` .... `Alt` + `Y`

    *NOTE: If one or more accounts are selected which
    you wish to deselect, click them in the
    Accounts Used box.*

14. Click **Transactions** .... `Alt` + `N`
    in **Customize** box.

15. Click **Amounts** box .... `Alt` + `M`

continued......

Account Balances Report (continued)

16. Choose one of the following **Amounts** options:

   - **All**

     Go to step 20.

   - **less than**

   - **equal to**

   - **greater than**

17. Click blank box to right of **Amounts** box.

18. Enter desired amount ....*amount*
    relative to option you chose in step 16.

   NOTE: *For example, if you want the report to
   display only transactions of less than fifty
   dollars, you would choose **less than** in
   step 16, and type 50 in step 18.*

19. Click **Tax–related Transactions Only** .. Alt + X
    if desired.

20. Click **Transaction Types** box .... Alt + T

21. Select desired transaction type.

22. Select/deselect one or more status options:

   - Blank

   - Newly Cleared

   - Reconciled

   NOTES: *The default values for the above options
   are preselected.*

         *To deselect any of the above options, click
   them.*

continue

Account Balances Report (continued)

23. Click **Show Rows**.............................. `Alt` + `R`

24. Click **Subcategories** box .... `Alt` + `S`

25. Select desired subcategories option from list.

26. Click **Categories/Classes**.................... `Alt` + `C`
    in **Customize** box.

27. Choose one of the following options:

    • Categories................................... `Alt` + `T`

    • Classes .... `Alt` + `S`

    NOTE: Categories is the default above.

28. Click each category or class to include in report
    from **Select to Include** box.

*If you have created more than seven classes, the Select to
Include box becomes a scroll box.*

OR

Click [**Mark All**] .... `Alt` + `M`

*NOTE: If one or more categories or classes are
          selected which you wish to deselect, click
          them in the **Select to Include** scroll box.*

29. Click **Matching** .... `Alt` + `G`
    in **Customize** box.

*Matching allows you to filter transactions appearing in reports
based on a specific characteristic of a payee, category, class,
memo or security.*

continued...

Account Balances Report (continued)

30. Select payee from box.

     OR

     a. Click **Payee Contains** box.............. `Alt` + `P`

     b. Type payee name .... *name*
        in dialog box.

31. Click **Category Contains** box .... `Alt` + `E`

32. Type category name .... *name*
    in dialog box.

     OR

     Select category from box.

33. Click **Class Contains** box.................... `Alt` + `S`

34. Type class name .... *name*
    in dialog box.

     OR

     Select class from box.

35. Click **Memo Contains** .... `Alt` + `M`
    and type memo.

36. Click [✔ **OK**] .... `↵`

ACCOUNTS PAYABLE BY VENDOR REPORT
Create A/P by Vendor Report

1. Click

2. Click **Business**.....................................**Alt** + **B**

3. Click **A/P by Vendor** .... **Tab**, **↓** **↑**

4. Click **Customize** ....**Alt** + **C**

5. Select desired report dates from **Report Dates** list.

    OR

    a. Click **from** box ....**Alt** + **F**
       and enter date.

    b. Click **to** box.................................**Alt** + **O**
       and enter date.

    *NOTE: At the **from** and **to** boxes, you can also*
    access the drop–down calendar from
    which you can select starting and ending
    dates.

6. Click **Title** box ....**Alt** + **I**

7. Type report title.. *title*

8. Click **Row** box...................................**Alt** + **W**

9. Select desired row headings from list.

continued...

Create A/P by Vendor Report (continued)

10. Click **Column** box.................................. `Alt` + `U`

11. Select desired column heading options.

12. Click **Organization** box .... `Alt` + `Z`

13. Choose one of the following organization options:
    - Income & expense
    - Cash flow basis

    If you want amounts rounded to nearest dollar:

    a. Deselect **Cents in Amounts**........... `Alt` + `S`

    b. Select **Amount as %**..................... `Alt` + `%`

14. Click **Accounts** .... `Alt` + `A`
    in **Customize** box.

15. Select each account to include in report from **Accounts Used** box.

    OR

    Click [🏦 **Mark All**] .... `Alt` + `M`

    OR

    Click one of the following **Accounts Used** buttons to select all accounts in that category:

    - [🏛 **Bank**] .... `Alt` + `B`

    - [🏦 **Cash**] .... `Alt` + `H`

contin►

Create A/P by Vendor Report (continued)

- **Credit Card** .... Alt + D
- **Investment** .... Alt + I
- **Asset** .... Alt + S
- **Liability** .... Alt + Y

> *NOTE: If one or more accounts are selected which you wish to deselect, click them in the **Accounts Used** box.*

16. Click **Transactions** .... Alt + N
in **Customize** box.

17. Click **Amounts** box .... Alt + M

18. Choose one of the following **Amounts** options:

- **All**

   Go to step 20.

- **less than**
- **equal to**
- **greater than**

19. Click blank box to right of **Amounts** box.

20. Enter desired amount .... *amount*
relative to option you
chose in step 17.

> *NOTE: For example, if you want the report to display only transactions of less than fifty dollars, you would choose **less than** in step 17, and type 50 in step 20.*

continued...

Create A/P by Vendor Report (continued)

21. Choose one or more of following options:

- Include Unrealized Gains .... Alt + U
- Tax–related Transactions Only ...... Alt + X

22. Click **Transaction Types** box .... Alt + T
and select desired type.

23. Select/deselect one or more status options:

- Blank
- Newly Cleared
- Reconciled

NOTES: The default values for the above options
are preselected.
To deselect any of the above options, click
them.

24. Click **Show Rows** .... Alt + R
in **Customize** box.

25. Click **Transfers** box............................. Alt + T

26. Click **Subcategories/Classes**............... Alt + S

27. Click **Categories/Classes** .... Alt + C
in **Customize** box.

28. Choose one of the following options:

- Categories .... Alt + T
- Classes.................................... Alt + S

NOTE: **Categories** is the default above.

continu

Create A/P by Vendor Report (continued)

29. Click each category or class to include in report from **Select to Include** box.

If you have created more than seven classes, the Select to Include box becomes a scroll box.

OR

Click 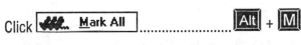 .... Alt + M

NOTE: *If one or more categories or classes are selected which you wish to deselect, click them in the Select to Include scroll box.*

30. Click **Matching** .... Alt + G
in **Customize** box.

Matching allows you to filter transactions appearing in reports based on a specific characteristic of a payee, category, class, memo or security.

31. Select payee from box.

OR

a. Click **Payee Contains** box .... Alt + P

b. Type payee name .... *name*
in dialog box.

32. Click **Category Contains** box .... Alt + E

33. Type category name .... *name*
in dialog box.

OR

Select category from box.

continued...

Create A/P by Vendor Report (continued)

34. Click **Class Contains** box..................... Alt + S

35. Type class name .... *name*
    in dialog box.

    OR

    Select class from box.

36. Click **Memo Contains** .... Alt + M
    and type memo.

37. Click [✔ OK] .... ⏎

ACCOUNTS RECEIVABLE BY CUSTOMER REPORT

Create A/R by Customer Report

1. Click

2. Click **Business**.....................................⬛B

3. Click **A/R by Customer**.

4. Click ▨ **Customize**.........................⬛Alt + ⬛C

5. Select desired report dates from **Report Dates** list.

    OR

    a. Click **from** box ....⬛Alt + ⬛F
        and enter date.

    b. Click **to** box.............................⬛Alt + ⬛O
        and enter date.

    NOTE: *At the **from** and **to** boxes, you can also*
             access the drop–down calendar from
             which you can select starting and ending
             dates.

6. Click **Title** box ....⬛Alt + ⬛I

7. Type report title .... *title*

8. Click **Row** box.

9. Select desired row heading option from list.

10. Click **Column** box.

11. Select desired column heading option from list.

continued...

Create A/R by Customer Report (continued)

12. Click **Organization** box .... Alt + Z

13. Choose one of the following organization options:

    - Income & expense

    - Cash flow basis

    If you want amounts rounded to nearest dollar:

    Deselect **Cents in Amounts** .... Alt + S

    If you want amounts displayed as percentage of whole:

    Select **Amount as %** .... Alt + %

14. Click **Accounts** .... Alt + A
    in **Customize** box.

15. Select each account to include in report from **Accounts Used** box.

    OR

    Click [💰 **Mark All**] .... Alt + M

    OR

    Choose one of the following **Accounts Used** buttons to select all accounts in that category:

    - [🏛 **Bank**] .... Alt + B

    - [💵 **Cash**] .... Alt + H

    - [CREDIT **Credit Card**] .... Alt + D

continu

Create A/R by Customer Report (continued)

- ![STOCK] **Investment** .... `Alt` + `I`

- ![house] **Asset** .... `Alt` + `S`

- ![car] **Liability** .... `Alt` + `Y`

> *NOTE: If one or more accounts are selected which you wish to deselect, click them in the **Accounts Used** box.*

16. Click **Transactions** .... `Alt` + `N`

17. Click **Amounts** box .... `Alt` + `M`

18. Choose one of the following **Amounts** options:

    - **All**

      Go to step 21.

    - **less than**

    - **equal to**

    - **greater than**

19. Click blank box to right of **Amounts** box.

20. Enter desired amount .... *amount* relative to option you chose in step 18.

    > *NOTE: For example, if you want the report to display only transactions of less than fifty dollars, you would choose **less than** in step 18, and enter 50 in step 20.*

    - Tax–related Transactions Only .... `Alt` + `X`

continued...

Create A/R by Customer Report (continued)

21. Choose one or more of following options:

- Include Underlined{U}nrealized Gains .... `Alt` + `U`

22. Click **Transaction Types** box .... `Alt` + `T`
and select desired type.

23. Select one or more of the following status options,
if desired:

- Blank .... `Alt` + `B`

- Newly Cleared .... `Alt` + `W`

- Reconciled .... `Alt` + `E`

*NOTES: The default values for the above options
are preselected.*

*To deselect any of above options, click
them.*

24. Click **Show Rows** .... `Alt` + `R`
in **Customize** box.

25. Click **Transfers** box............................... `Alt` + `T`

26. Select desired transfers option from list.

27. Click **Subcategories** box....................... `Alt` + `S`
and select desired subcategories.

28. Click **Categories/Classes** .... `Alt` + `C`

continu

Create A/R by Customer Report (continued)

29. Choose one of the following options:

- Categories.......................................**Alt** + **E**

- Classes ....**Alt** + **S**

    NOTE: **Categories** *is the default above.*

30. Click each category or class to include in report from **Select to Include** box.

    OR

    Click **Mark All** ....**Alt** + **M**

    NOTE: *If one or more categories or classes are selected which you wish to deselect, click them in the **Select to Include** scroll box.*

31. Click **Matching** ....**Alt** + **G**
    in **Customize** box.

    Matching allows you to filter transactions appearing in reports based on a specific characteristic of a payee, category, class, memo or security.

32. Click **Payee Contains** box ....**Alt** + **P**

33. Type payee name.. *name*
    in dialog box.

    OR

    Select payee from box.

34. Click **Category Contains** box...............**Alt** + **E**

35. Type category name .... *name*
    in dialog box.

continued...

Create A/R by Customer Report (continued)

    OR

    Select category from box.

36. Click **Class Contains** box...................... Alt + S

37. Type class name .... *name*
    in dialog box.

    OR

    Select class from box.

38. Type memo...*memo*
    in **Memo Contains** dialog box.

39. Click [✔ OK] .... ⏎

BACK UP QUICKEN FILES

Back Up Current File to Formatted Diskette

1. Click **File** .... Alt + F
2. Click **Backup** .... B
3. Insert floppy diskette into floppy drive.

   —IN FILE TO BACK UP SECTION—

4. Click **Current File** .... Alt + C

   OR

   Click **Select from List** .... Alt + S

5. Press **Tab** .... Tab
6. Type drive letter .... *letter*
7. Click ✔ **OK** .... ↵

   If you chose Select from List in step 4:

   a. Click appropriate file.

      OR

      Type desired filename .... *name*

   b. Click ✔ **OK** .... ↵

BALANCE SHEET REPORT

Create Balance Sheet Report

1. Click **Reports**

2. Click **Business** .... **B**

3. Click **Balance Sheet**.

4. Click **Customize** .... **Alt** + **C**

5. Select desired report dates from **Report Dates** list.

   OR

   a. Click **from** box.............................. **Alt** + **F**
      and enter date.

   b. Click **to** box .... **Alt** + **O**
      and enter date.

   *NOTE: At the **from** and **to** boxes, you can also
   access the drop–down calendar from
   which you can select starting and ending
   dates.*

6. Click **Title** box.............................. **Alt** + **I**

7. Type report title .... *title*

8. Click **Interval** box .... **Alt** + **V**

9. Select desired interval for column headings from
   list.

continu

Create Balance Sheet Report (continued)

10. Click **Organization** box...................... **Alt** + **Z**

11. Choose one of the following organization options:

    - Balance sheet

    - Net Worth

    If you do not want amounts rounded to nearest dollar:

    Select **Show Cents in Amounts**........... **Alt** + **S**

12. Click **Accounts**................................... **Alt** + **A**
    in **Customize** box.

13. Select each account to include in report from **Accounts Used** box.

    OR

    Click [**Mark All**] .... **Alt** + **M**

    OR

    Choose one of the following **Accounts Used** buttons to select all accounts in that category:

    - [**Bank**] .... **Alt** + **B**

    - [**Cash**] .... **Alt** + **H**

    - [**Credit Card**] .... **Alt** + **D**

    - [**Investment**] .... **Alt** + **I**

    - [**Asset**] .... **Alt** + **S**

Create Balance Sheet Report (continued)

- | 🚗 **Liability** | .... **Alt** + **Y**

  NOTE: *If one or more accounts are selected which you wish to deselect, click them in the* **Accounts Used** *box.*

14. Click **Transactions**.............................. **Alt** + **N**
    in **Customize** box.

15. Click **Amounts** box.............................. **Alt** + **M**

16. Choose one of the following **Amounts** options:

    - **All**

      Go to step 19.
    - **less than**
    - **equal to**
    - **greater than**

17. Click blank box to right of **Amounts** box.

18. Enter desired amount ....*amount*
    relative to option you
    chose in step 16.

    NOTE: *For example, if you want the report to display only transactions of less than fifty dollars, you would choose* **less than** *in step 16, and type* 50 *in step 18.*

19. Choose one or more of the following options, if desired:

    - Include Unrealized Gains................ **Alt** + **U**

    - Tax-related Transactions Only........ **Alt** + **X**

contin

Create Balance Sheet Report (continued)

20. Click **Transaction Types** box................ `Alt` + `T`

21. Select desired transaction type to appear in report from list.

22. Select one or more of the following status options, if desired:

- Blank .... `Alt` + `B`

- Newly Cleared................................... `Alt` + `W`

- Reconciled....................................... `Alt` + `E`

    NOTES: The default values for the above options are preselected.

    To deselect any of the above options, click them.

23. Click **Show Rows**................................... `Alt` + `R`
    in **Customize** box.

24. Click **Subcategories** box .... `Alt` + `S`

25. Select desired subcategories option from list.

26. Click **Categories/Classes**..................... `Alt` + `C`
    in **Customize** box.

27. Choose one of the following options:

- Categories .... `Alt` + `E`

- Classes .... `Alt` + `S`

    *NOTE: **Categories** is the default selection above.*

continued...

40

28. Click each category or class to include in report from **Select to Include** box.

For categories, the Select to Include box is a scroll box. If you have created more than seven classes, the Select to Include box also becomes a scroll box.

OR

Click [**Mark All**] .... [Alt] + [M]

> NOTE: *If one or more categories or classes are selected which you wish to deselect, click them in the Select to Include scroll box.*

29. Click **Matching**................................... [Alt] + [G]
    in **Customize** box.

Matching allows you to filter transactions appearing in reports based on a specific characteristic of a payee, category, class, memo or security.

30. Click **Payee Contains** box.................... [Alt] + [P]

31. Type payee name.. *name*
    in dialog box.

32. Click **Category Contains** box .... [Alt] + [E]

33. Type category name .... *name*
    in dialog box.

34. Click **Class Contains** box.................... [Alt] + [S]

35. Type class name .... *name*
    in dialog box.

36. Click **Memo Contains** dialog box.......... [Alt] + [M]
    and type memo.

37. Click [✔ **OK**] .... [↵]

BILLMINDER

Turn On Billminder

1. Click **Options** .... Alt + E , O

2. Click **Reminders** .... Alt + E

3. Select/deselect desired options:

   - Turn on Billminder .... Alt + T

   - Enter number of days in advance .... *number*

   - Show Reminder on Startup .... Alt + S

   - Show Calendar Notes .... Alt + C

4. Click **✔ OK** .... ⏎

BUDGET

Set Up Budget Amounts for Categories

1. Click **Plan** .... Alt + A

2. Click **Budgeting** .... B

3. Enter budget amounts .... *amounts*
   in any or all monthly columns.

4. Click **Close**

5. Click **✔ Yes** .... Alt + Y
   to save budgets.

   OR

continued...

Set Up Budget Amounts for Categories (continued)

Click | ⊘　　**N**o | .... Alt + N

to exit budget window without saving changes.

OR

Click | ✖　Cancel | .... Esc

to return to budget window.

Autocreate Budget

Enters budget amounts automatically, based on existing account data.

1. Click **Pl**a**n** .... Alt + A

2. Click **B**udgeting .... B

3. Click | 🖑 **C**reate | .... Alt + C

Automatically Create Budget

Transactions
From: 1/93   To: 12/93

Amounts
Round Values to Nearest $1

◯ Use Monthly **D**etail
◉ Use **A**verage for Period

✔ OK
✖ Cancel
📖 **C**ategories...
❓ Help

4. Click **F**rom box................................. Alt + F
and enter date.

5. Click **T**o box...................................... Alt + O
and enter date.

contin

6. Select value from **Round Values to Nearest** list.

7. Choose one of the following options:

   • Use Monthly Detail .... `Alt` + `D`

   • Use Average for Period.................... `Alt` + `A`

8. Click [Categories...] .... `Alt` + `C`

9. Select desired category or categories from **Categories** scroll box.

10. Click desired categories to mark or unmark.

    OR

    Click [Mark All] .... `Alt` + `M`

    OR

    Click [Clear All] .... `Alt` + `L`
    and then select individual accounts.

11. Click [✔ OK] .... `↵`

Edit Budget Spreadsheet

1. Click **Pl_a_n** .... Alt + A

2. Click **_B_udgeting** .... B

3. Click amount in category and under month to edit.

4. Click [⬜ Edit] .... Alt + D

5. Choose from the following options:

- **2–_W_eek** .... W
  to set up an item occurring at two week
  intervals.

  a. Enter amount to budget .... *amount*
     in **_A_mount** box.

  b. Press **Tab** .... Tab

  c. Enter beginning date .... *date*
     in **_E_very two weeks starting** box.

  d. Click [✔ OK] .... ↵

- **Co_p_y All** .... P
  to copy budget to Windows
  clipboard for insertion into
  other programs, using their
  paste commands.

- **Clear R_o_w** .... O
  to clear row of budget
  amounts for selected category.

  Click [✔ Yes] .... Y

continu

Edit Budget Spreadsheet (continued)

- **Clear All Budgets**.....................................  L
  to clear budget amounts
  for all categories and periods.

  Click [✔ Yes]..................................... Y

- **Fill Row Right**... R
  to copy amount to all cells
  to right in same row.

  Click [✔ Yes]..................................... Y

- **Fill Columns**.. C
  to copy amounts in one
  column to all columns on right.

  Click [✔ Yes]..................................... Y

- **Supercategories**.................................... S
  to group categories for budgeting categories.

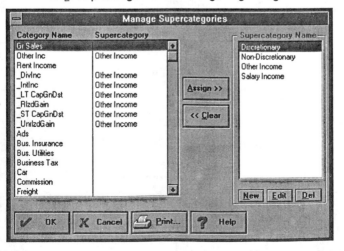

continued...

Edit Budget Spreadsheet (continued)

To assign category to supercategory:

a. Click category on left.

b. Click supercategory on right.

c. Click <u>A</u>ssign >> .... `Alt` + `A`

Layout Budget Spreadsheet

Designs spreadsheet layout.

1. Click **Pl<u>a</u>n** .... `Alt` + `A`

2. Click **<u>B</u>udgeting** .... `B`

3. Click Layout .... `Alt` + `Y`

4. Choose one of the following **Columns** designations:

    - **<u>M</u>onth** .... `Alt` + `M`
      to organize budgets monthly.

    - **<u>Q</u>uarter** .... `Alt` + `Q`
      to organize budgets quarterly.

    - **<u>Y</u>ear** .... `Alt` + `Y`
      to organize budgets annually.

    If you want to enter budget amounts for Supercategories:

    Click **Sho<u>w</u> S<u>u</u>percategories** .... `Alt` + `U`

    If you want to enter budget amounts for transfers:

    Click **Show <u>T</u>ransfers** .... `Alt` + `T`

    If you want to hide unbudgeted categories:

    Click **<u>H</u>ide Zero Budget Categories** ..... `Alt` + `H`

5. Click ✔ OK .... `↵`

Print Budget

1. Click **Pla̲n** .... `Alt` + `A`

2. Click **B̲udgeting** .... `B`

3. Click [🖶 Pri̲nt] .... `Alt` + `N`

4. Choose one of the following **Print to** options:

   - Pr̲inter .... `Alt` + `R`

   - ASCII D̲isk File .... `Alt` + `D`

   - Ta̲b–delimited Disk File .... `Alt` + `B`

   - 1̲23 [.PRN] Disk File .... `Alt` + `1`

5. Choose one or more of the following options, if desired:

   - Print in c̲olor .... `Alt` + `C`

   - Print in draft m̲ode .... `Alt` + `M`

6. Choose one of the following **Print Range** options:

   - **A̲ll** .... `Alt` + `A`

   - **Pa̲ges** .... `Alt` + `G`

     a. Click **F̲rom** box .... `Alt` + `F`
        and enter number.

     b. Click **T̲o** box............................. `Alt` + `T`
        and enter number.

7. Click [🖶 Pri̲nt] .... `Alt` + `P`

Save Budget

1. Click **Pl<u>a</u>n** .... `Alt` + `A`

2. Click **<u>B</u>udgeting** .... `B`

3. Create your budget using **<u>C</u>reate**, **E<u>d</u>it** and **La<u>y</u>out** commands.

4. Click **📝 <u>S</u>ave** .... `Alt` + `S`

Restore Budget

Restores budget to its previously saved condition, or to how it was when you opened it.

1. Click **Pl<u>a</u>n** .... `Alt` + `A`

2. Click **<u>B</u>udgeting** .... `B`

3. Create or alter your budget using **<u>C</u>reate**, **E<u>d</u>it** and **La<u>y</u>out** commands.

4. Click **📇 Res<u>t</u>ore** .... `Alt` + `T`

5. Click **<u>Y</u>es** .... `Alt` + `Y`

Close Budget

1. Click **Pl<u>a</u>n** .... `Alt` + `A`

2. Click **<u>B</u>udgeting** .... `B`

3. Create or alter your budget using **<u>C</u>reate**, **E<u>d</u>it** and **La<u>y</u>out** commands.

4. Click **🚪 Close**

BUDGET REPORT

Create Budget Report

1. Click **Reports**

2. Click **Other** .... **Alt** + **E**

3. Click **Budget** .... **Tab** + **↓** **↑**

4. Click **Customize** .... **Alt** + **C**

The Customize Budget Report window appears. It will only display options applying to the report you are creating.

5. Select desired report dates from **Report Dates** list.

   OR

   a. Click **from** box .... **Alt** + **F**
      and enter start date.

   b. Click **to** box.................................. **Alt** + **O**
      and enter ending date.

   *NOTE: At the **from** and **to** boxes, you can also access the drop–down calendar from which you can select starting and ending dates.*

6. Click **Title** box .... **Alt** + **I**
   in **Reports Layout** area.

7. Type report title... *title*

8. Click **Column** box .... **Alt** + **U**

continued...

Create Budget Report (continued)

9. Select interval for column headings from list.

10. Click **Organization** box .... `Alt` + `Z`

11. Choose one of the following **Organization** options:

    - Income & Expense

    - Cash flow basis

    - Supercategory

    If you do not want amounts rounded to nearest dollar:

    Deselect **Show Cents in Amounts** .... `Alt` + `S`

12. Click **Accounts** .... `Alt` + `A`
    in **Customize** box.

13. Select each account to include in report from **Accounts Used** box.

    OR

    Click [**Mark All**] .... `Alt` + `M`

    OR

    Click one of following **Accounts Used** buttons to select all accounts in that category:

    - [🏦 **Bank**] .... `Alt` + `B`

    - [💵 **Cash**] .... `Alt` + `H`

    - [**Credit Card**] .... `Alt` + `D`

continue

Create Budget Report (continued)

- `[STOCK] Investment` .... `Alt` + `I`

- `[🏠] Asset` .... `Alt` + `S`

- `[🚗] Liability` .... `Alt` + `Y`

   *NOTE: If one or more accounts are selected which
   you wish to deselect, click them in the
   Accounts Used box.*

14. Click **Transactions** .... `Alt` + `N`
    in **Customize** box.

15. Click **Amounts** box .... `Alt` + `M`

16. Choose one of the following **Amounts** options:

    - **All**

       Go to step 19.

    - **less than**

    - **equal to**

    - **greater than**

17. Click blank box to right of **Amounts** box.

18. Enter desired amount .... *amount*
    relative to option
    you chose in step 16.

   *NOTE: For example, if you want the report to
   display only transactions of less than fifty
   dollars, you would choose **less than** in
   step 16, and type 50 in step 18.*

continued...

Create Budget Report (continued)

19. Choose one or more of the following options, if desired:

- Include Underlized Gains .... **Alt** + **U**

- Tax–related Transactions Only ...... **Alt** + **X**

20. Click **Transaction Types** box .... **Alt** + **T**

21. Select desired **Transaction Types** to appear in report from list.

22. Select one or more of the following status options, if desired:

- Blank .... **Alt** + **B**

- Newly Cleared .... **Alt** + **W**

- Reconciled .... **Alt** + **E**

    NOTES: The default values for the above options are preselected.

23. Click **Show Rows** .... **Alt** + **R** in **Customize** box.

24. Click **Transfers** box............................. **Alt** + **T**

25. Select desired **Transfers** option from list.

26. Click **Subcategories** box...................... **Alt** + **S**

27. Select desired **Subcategories** option from list.

28. Click **Categories** box .... **Alt** + **E**

continu

Create Budget Report (continued)

29. Select desired **Categories** option from list.

30. Click **Categories/Classes** .... Alt + C
    in **Customize** box.

31. Choose one of the following options:

    • Categories .... Alt + E

    • Classes .... Alt + S

    NOTE: *Categories is the default selection above.*

32. Click each category or class to include in report
    from **Select to Include** box.

    OR

    Click  .... Alt + M

    NOTE: *If one or more categories or classes are*
    selected which you wish to deselect, click
    *them in the **Select to Include** scroll box.*

    OR

    Click  .... Alt + E
    then select desired accounts.

continued...

54

Create Budget Report (continued)

33. Click **Matching**.................................. `Alt` + `G`
    in **Customize** box.

*Matching allows you to filter transactions appearing in reports
based on a specific characteristic of a payee, category, class,
memo or security.*

34. Click **Payee Contains** box.................... `Alt` + `P`
    and type payee name.

    OR

    Select payee from box.

35. Click **Category Contains** box............... `Alt` + `E`
    and type and name.

    OR

    Select category from box.

36. Click **Class Contains** box..................... `Alt` + `S`
    and type and name.

    OR

    Select class from box.

37. Click **Memo Contains** dialog box......... `Alt` + `M`
    and type memo.

38. Click [✔ **OK**] .... `↵`

CALCULATOR

Use Calculator

1. Click  .... **Alt** + **V**, **A**

   NOTE: *To add **Use Calculator** button to iconbar,*
   *follow instructions in **Add New Icon to***
   ***Iconbar**, page 126.*

2. Click first number for calculation.

3. Choose one of the following functions:

   - **+** (plus) .... **+**

   - **−** (minus) .... **−**

   - ***** (multiply) .... *****

   - **/** (divide) .... **/**

continued...

56

Use Calculator (continued)

4. Click second number of calculation.

    *NOTE: If the calculation requires more than two
    numbers, repeat steps 2–3 for each
    additional number before going to step 4.*

5. Click = (equals) ....

Calculation is performed.

To paste calculation:

a. Select desired destination.

b. Click

CAPITAL GAINS INVESTMENT REPORT

Create Capital Gains Investment Report

1. Click Reports

2. Click **Investment**............................... Alt + I

3. Click **Capital Gains**....................... Tab , ↓ ↑

4. Click Customize .... Alt + C

continu

Create Capital Gains Investment Report (continued)

5. Select desired report dates from **Report Dates** list.

   OR

   a. Click **from** box .... Alt + F
      and enter date.

   b. Click **to** box .... Alt + O
      and enter date.

   NOTE: *At the **from** and **to** boxes, you can also access the drop–down calendar from which you can select starting and ending dates.*

6. Click **Title** box .... Alt + I

7. Type report title .... *title*

8. Click **Subtotal By** box .... Alt + U

9. Select subtotal option from list.

10. Click **Max Short–Term Gain** .... Alt + H
    Holding Period box.

11. Enter number .... *number*
    of days in period.

12. Click **Organization box** .... Alt + Z

13. Choose one of the following **Organization** options:

    • Income and Expense

    • Cash flow basis

continued...

Create Capital Gains Investment Report (continued)

If you do not want amounts rounded to nearest dollar:

Click **Show Cents in Amounts** .... `Alt` + `S`

14. Click **Accounts** .... `Alt` + `A`
    in **Customize** box.

15. Select each account to include in report from **Accounts Used** box.

    OR

    Click [🎀 **Mark All**] .... `Alt` + `M`

    OR

    Choose one of the following category buttons to select all accounts in that category:

- [🏛 **Bank**] .... `Alt` + `B`

- [💵 **Cash**] .... `Alt` + `H`

- [💳 **Credit Card**] .... `Alt` + `D`

- [📈 **Investment**] .... `Alt` + `I`

- [🏠 **Asset**] .... `Alt` + `S`

- [🚗 **Liability**] .... `Alt` + `Y`

NOTE: If one or more accounts are selected which you wish to deselect, click them in the **Accounts Used** *box.*

continu

Create Capital Gains Investment Report (continued)

16. Click **Transactions** .... `Alt` + `N`
    in **Customize** box.

17. Choose one or more of the following options, if
    desired:

    - Include Unrealized Gains............... `Alt` + `U`

    - Tax–related Transactions Only....... `Alt` + `X`

18. Select one or more of the following status options,
    if desired:

    - Blank.. `Alt` + `B`

    - Newly Cleared .... `Alt` + `W`

    - Reconciled .... `Alt` + `E`

    *NOTES: The default values for the above options
    are preselected.*

19. Click **Show Rows**.............................. `Alt` + `R`
    in **Customize** box.

20. Click **Transfers** box .... `Alt` + `T`

21. Select desired **Transfers** option from list.

22. Click **Select to Include** .... `Alt` + `C`

23. Choose one of the following **Select to Include**
    options:

    - Securities...................................... `Alt` + `S`

    - Security Types .... `Alt` + `T`

    - Investment Goals.......................... `Alt` + `V`

continued...

Create Capital Gains Investment Report (continued)

24. Click each **Select to Include** option to include in report from **Select to Include** box.

    OR

    Click [**Mark All**] .... [Alt] + [M]

    NOTE: *If one or more options are selected which you wish to deselect, click them in the* **Select to Include** *scroll box.*

    OR

    Click [**Clear All**] .... [Alt] + [E]

25. Click **Matching**................................ [Alt] + [G]
    in **Customize** box.

    Matching allows you to filter transactions appearing in reports based on a specific characteristic of a payee, category, class, memo or security.

26. Click **Security Contains** .... [Alt] + [Y]

27. Type security name....................................... *name*
    in dialog box.

    OR

    Select security from box.

28. Click [✔ **OK**] .... [↵]

CASH FLOW BUSINESS REPORT

Create Cash Flow Business Report

1. Click ⊞ Reports

2. Click **Business**...................................... **Alt** + **B**

3. Click **Cash Flow**.

4. Click 🔨 **Customize** .... **Alt** + **C**

5. Select desired report dates from **Report Dates** list.

   OR

   a. Click **from** box .... **Alt** + **F**
      and enter date.

   b. Click **to** box............................... **Alt** + **O**
      and enter date.

   *NOTE: At the **from** and **to** boxes, you can also
   access the drop–down calendar from
   which you can select starting and ending
   dates.*

6. Click **Title** box .... **Alt** + **I**

7. Type report title .... *title*

8. Click **Row** box.................................... **Alt** + **W**

9. Select desired row heading option from list.

10. Click **Column** box .... **Alt** + **U**

11. Select desired column heading option from list.

12. Click **Organization** box........................ **Alt** + **Z**

continued...

Create Cash Flow Business Report (continued)

13. Choose one of the following **Organization** options:

    - Income & expense
    - Cash flow basis

    If you do not want amounts rounded to nearest dollar:

    Click **Show Cents in Amounts** .... `Alt` + `S`

    If you want amounts displayed as percentage of the whole:

    Click **Amount as %** .... `Alt` + `%`

14. Click **Accounts** .... `Alt` + `A`
    in **Customize** box.

15. Select each account to include in report from **Accounts Used** box.

    OR

    Click ▟ **Mark All** .... `Alt` + `M`

    OR
    Choose one of the following **Accounts Used** buttons to select all accounts in that category:

    - 🏛 **Bank** .... `Alt` + `B`

    - 🏚 **Cash** .... `Alt` + `H`

    - 💳 **Credit Card** .... `Alt` + `D`

    - 📈 **Investment** .... `Alt` + `I`

    - 🏠 **Asset** .... `Alt` + `S`

    - 🚗 **Liability** .... `Alt` + `Y`

continue

Create Cash Flow Business Report (continued)

> *NOTE:* *If one or more accounts are selected which you wish to deselect, click them in the **Accounts Used** box.*

16. Click **Transactions** .... Alt + N
    in **Customize** box.

17. Click **Amounts** box .... Alt + M

18. Choose one of the following **Amounts** options:

    - **All**

      Go to step 21.

    - **less than**

    - **equal to**

    - **greater than**

19. Click blank box to right of **Amounts** box.

20. Enter desired amount .... *amount*
    relative to option
    you chose in step 18.

    > *NOTE:* *For example, if you want the report to display only transactions of less than fifty dollars, you would choose **less than** in step 18, and enter 50 in step 20.*

21. Choose one or more of the following options, if desired:

    - Include Unrealized Gains................ Alt + U

    - Tax–related Transactions Only....... Alt + X

continued...

Create Cash Flow Business Report (continued)

22. Click **Transaction Types** box .... `Alt` + `T`

23. Select desired transaction type to appear in report from list.

24. Select one or more of the following status options, if desired:

    - Blank .... `Alt` + `B`

    - Newly Cleared .... `Alt` + `W`

    - Reconciled .... `Alt` + `E`

    NOTES: The default values for the above options are preselected.

25. Click **Show Rows** .... `Alt` + `R`
    in **Customize** box.

26. Click **Transfers** box.............................. `Alt` + `T`

27. Select desired **Transfers** option from list.

28. Click **Subcategories** box...................... `Alt` + `S`

29. Select desired **Subcategories** option from list.

30. Click **Categories/Classes** .... `Alt` + `C`

31. Choose one of the following options:

    - Categories .... `Alt` + `T`

    - Classes.. `Alt` + `S`

    *NOTE: **Categories** is the default above.*

continu

Create Cash Flow Business Report (continued)

32. Click each category or class to include in report
    from **Select to Include** box.

    OR

    Click [*** **M**ark All] .... `Alt` + `M`

    *NOTE: If one or more categories or classes are
    selected which you wish to deselect, click
    them in the **Select to Include** scroll box.*

33. Click **Matching** .... `Alt` + `G`
    in **Customize** box.

*Matching allows you to filter transactions appearing in reports
based on a specific characteristic of a payee, category, class,
memo or security.*

34. Click **Payee Contains** box .... `Alt` + `P`

35. Type payee name... *name*
    in dialog box.

36. Click **Category Contains** box............... `Alt` + `E`

37. Type category name .... *name*
    in dialog box.

38. Click **Class Contains** box .... `Alt` + `S`

39. Type class name... *name*
    in dialog box.

40. Press **Tab** .... `Tab`

41. Type memo .... *memo*
    in **Memo Contains** dialog box.

42. Click [✔ OK] .... `↵`

CASH FLOW HOME REPORT

Create Cash Flow Home Report

1. Click **Reports**

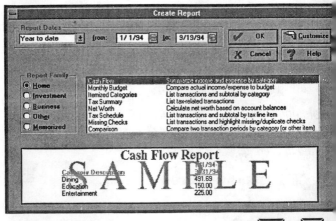

2. Click **Home** .... `Alt` + `H`

3. Click **Cash Flow** .... `Tab`, `↓` `↑`

4. Click **Customize** .... `Alt` + `C`

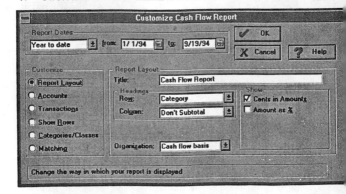

continu▸

Create Cash Flow Home Report (continued)

5. Select desired report dates from **Report Dates** list.

   OR

   a. Click **from** box .... Alt + F
   and enter date.

   b. Click **to** box .... Alt + O
   and enter date.

   *NOTE: At the **from** and **to** boxes, you can also access the drop–down calendar from which you can select starting and ending dates.*

6. Click **Title** box .... Alt + I

7. Type report title .... *title*

8. Click **Row** box .... Alt + W

9. Select desired row heading option from list.

10. Click **Column** box .... Alt + U

11. Select desired column heading option from list.

12. Click **Organization** box .... Alt + Z

13. Choose one of the following organization options:

    • Income & expense

    • Cash flow basis

    If you do not want amounts rounded to nearest dollar:

continued...

68

Create Cash Flow Home Report (continued)

Deselect **Show Cents in Amount**<u>s</u>........ `Alt` + `S`

If you want amounts displayed as percentage of whole:

Select **Amount as <u>%</u>**.......................... `Alt` + `%`

14. Click <u>A</u>**ccounts**...................................... `Alt` + `A`
    in **Customize** box.

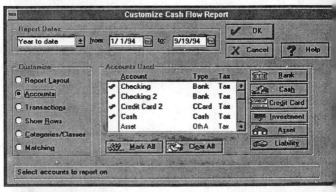

15. Select each account to include in report from **Accounts Used** box.

    OR

    Click [**Mark All**]........................ `Alt` + `M`

    OR

    Choose one of the following **Accounts Used** buttons to select all accounts in that category:

continu

Create Cash Flow Home Report (continued)

- | 🏦 **B**ank | .... | Alt + B |

- | 🏠 **Cas**h | .... | Alt + H |

- | 💳 **Cre**dit Card | .... | Alt + D |

- | 📈 **I**nvestment | .... | Alt + I |

- | 🏠 **A**sset | .... | Alt + S |

- | 🚗 **Liabilit**y | .... | Alt + Y |

> *NOTE:* *If one or more accounts are selected which you wish to deselect, click them in the* ***Accounts Used*** *box.*

16. Click **Transactio**n**s** .... Alt + N
    in **Customize** box.

17. Click **A**m**ounts** box .... Alt + M

18. Choose one of the following **A**m**ounts** options:

    - **All**

      Go to step 21.

    - **less than**

    - **equal to**

    - **greater than**

19. Click blank box to right of **A**m**ounts** box.

20. Enter desired amount .... *amount*
    relative to option you chose in step 18.

    > *NOTE:* *For example, if you want the report to display only transactions of less than fifty dollars, you would choose **less than** in step 18, and type* 50 *in step 20.*

continued......

Create Cash Flow Home Report (continued)

21. Choose one or more of the following options, if desired:

    - Include <u>U</u>nrealized Gains .... `Alt` + `U`

    - Ta<u>x</u>–related Transactions Only ...... `Alt` + `X`

22. Click **Transaction Types** box .... `Alt` + `T`

23. Select desired transaction type to appear in report from list.

24. Select one or more of the following status options, if desired:

    - <u>B</u>lank .... `Alt` + `B`

    - Ne<u>w</u>ly Cleared .... `Alt` + `W`

    - R<u>e</u>conciled .... `Alt` + `E`

    NOTE: The default values for the above options are preselected.

25. Click **Show Rows** .... `Alt` + `R` in **Customize** box.

26. Click **Transfers** box............................. `Alt` + `T`

27. Select desired transfers option from list.

28. Click **Subcategories** box....................... `Alt` + `S`

29. Select desired subcategories option from list.

continu

Create Cash Flow Home Report (continued)

30. Click **Categories/Classes** .... `Alt` + `C`
    in **Customize** box.

31. Choose one of the following options:

    • Categories .... `Alt` + `T`

    • Classes .... `Alt` + `S`

    NOTE: Categories is the default above.

32. Click each category or class to include in report
    from **Select to Include** box.

    OR

    Click ⟦ **Mark All** ⟧ .... `Alt` + `M`

    *NOTE: If one or more categories or classes are
    selected which you wish to deselect, click
    them in the **Select to Include** scroll box.*

33. Click **Matching** .... `Alt` + `G`
    in **Customize** box.

    *Matching allows you to filter transactions appearing in reports
    based on a specific characteristic of a payee, category, class,
    memo or security.*

34. Click **Payee Contains** box .... `Alt` + `P`

35. Type payee name .... *name*
    in dialog box.

    OR

    Select payee from box.

continued...

72

Create Cash Flow Home Report (continued)

36. Click **Category Contains** box .... `Alt` + `E`

37. Type category name .... *name*
    in dialog box.

    OR

    Select category from box.

38. Click **Class Contains** box .... `Alt` + `S`

39. Type class name .... *name*
    in dialog box.

    OR

    Select class from box.

40. Press **Tab** .... `Tab`

41. Click **Memo Contains** dialog box .... `Alt` + `M`
    and type memo.

42. Click ✔ **OK** .... `↵`

CATEGORIES

Assign Category to Transaction

1. Click **Activities** .... Ctrl + W

2. Type transaction information in **Write Checks** window.

   *NOTE: Press **Tab** to move around the various input fields in the **Write Checks** window.*

   —IN CATEGORY FIELD—

3. Type category name .... *name*

   To select category from list:

   a. Click down arrow to open list.

      To find category name:

      Scroll up and down list .... ↑ ↓

   b. Click appropriate category.

4. Click ⌐Recon .... Alt + C

   NOTE: You can assign a category to a transaction via the Register as well as the Write Checks window.

Create New Category

1. Click **Lists** .... Alt + L , C

2. Click [➕ New] .... Alt + N

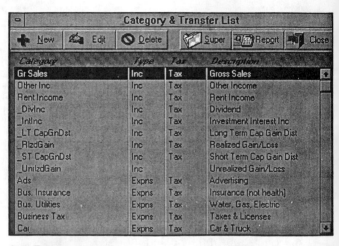

3. Type category name .... *name*

4. Press **Tab** .... Tab

5. Type description .... *description*
   if desired.

6. Choose one of the following category types:

   • Income .... Alt + I

   • Expense .... Alt + E

   • Subcategory of .... Alt + U

continu

If you selected subcategory:

Type category name .... *name* of which it is a subcategory.

OR

a.   Click arrow to open list.

b.   Scroll list to find category name.

c.   Click appropriate category.

If category (or subcategory) is tax related:

Click **Tax Related** box .... `Alt` + `T`

7.   Click [✔ OK] .... `↵`

Delete Category

1.   Click **Lists**................................. `Alt` + `L`, `C`

2.   Highlight category .... `Tab`, `↓` `↑`
     to delete.

3.   Click [🚫 Delete] .... `Alt` + `D`

4.   Click [✔ OK] .... `↵`

> *NOTE: If you are deleting a subcategory, a
>   message will warn you that all transactions
>   assigned to the subcategory will be
>   merged to the parent category. Click **Yes**.*

Edit Category

1. Click **Lists** .... Alt + L , C

2. Highlight category .... Tab , ↓ ↑
   to delete.

3. Click Edit .... Alt + I

4. Make necessary changes to category name, description and/or type.

5. Click ✔ OK .... ↵

CHECKFREE

Pays bills electronically. To get started with Quicken's CheckFree feature, please see the Quicken User's Guide. CheckFree requires the use of a Hayes–compatible modem; and you must also pay a monthly subscription fee.

Set Up Bank Account for Electronic Payments

1. Click **Activities** .... Alt + V

2. Click **CheckFree** .... K

3. Click **Setup** .... S

continu

Set Up Bank Account for Electronic Payments
(continued)

4. Highlight bank account............................ ⬇ ⬆
   to set up.

5. Click ✔ Set Up

6. Click **Enable Electronic Payments**....... Alt + E
   for Account "X".

   NOTE: *If there is already a check in the box, go*
   directly to step 7.

7. Press **Tab** .... Tab

8. Type your first name .... *name*

9. Press **Tab** .... Tab

10. Type your middle initial (optional) .... *initial*

11. Press **Tab** .... Tab

12. Type your last name .... *name*

13. Press **Tab** .... Tab

14. Type your street address ....*address*

15. Press **Tab** .... Tab

16. Type your city.. *city*

17. Press **Tab** .... Tab

18. Type your state initials .... *initials*

19. Press **Tab** .... Tab

20. Enter your zip code.................................. *zip code*

continued...

Set Up Bank Account for Electronic Payments (continued)

21. Press **Tab** .... Tab
22. Enter your home phone number .... *number*

23. Press **Tab** .... Tab
24. Enter your CheckFree account number ...... *number*

25. Press **Tab** .... Tab
26. Enter your CheckFree security code .... *code*
27. Click [✔ OK] .... ↵

Set or Change Modem Settings

1. Click **Acti̱vities** .... Alt + V

2. Click **Chec̱kFree** C

3. Click **Set Up M̱odem** .... M

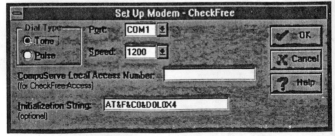

If you have a touchtone phone:

Click **Ṯone** .... Alt + T

If you have a rotary phone:

Click **P̱ulse** .... Alt + P

continu

Set or Change Modem Settings (continued)

—IN PORT BOX—

4. Click down arrow to select from **P̲ort** list.

5. Choose one of the port settings.

—IN SPEED BOX—

6. Click down arrow.................................... [↓]
   to select from **speed** list.

7. Choose one of the modem speeds:

8. Press **Tab** .... [Tab]

9. Enter **C̲ompuServe local access number** *..number*

10. Press **Tab** .... [Tab]

11. Type initialization string............................*string*

    NOTE: The above step is optional.

12. Click [✔ OK] .... [↵]

Transmit Electronic Check

NOTE: Write and record Electronic Payments
before attempting to transmit them.

1. Click **Acti̲vities** .... [Alt] + [V]

2. Click **Chec̲kFree** .... [K]

3. Click **T̲ransmit** .... [T]

4. Click [⚡ T̲ransmit] .... [Alt] + [T]

continued......

Transmit Electronic Check (continued)

To select from list of checks to transmit:

a. Click **P**review .... `Alt` + `P`

b. Select (highlight) check to transmit.

c. Click **T**ransmit .... `Alt` + `T`

Write Electronic Check

1. Click **Acti**v**ities** .... `Alt` + `V`

2. Click **W**rite Checks .... `W`

3. Enter check date .... *date*

4. Press **Tab** .... `Tab`

5. Type payee name .... *name*

6. Press **Tab** .... `Tab`

   To select payee from list:

   a. Click down arrow .... `↓`

   b. Click desired payee.

7. Enter check dollar amount .... *amount*

8. Press **Tab** .... `Tab`

9. Type memo .... *memo*

   NOTE: *The above step is optional.*

10. Press **Tab** .... `Tab`

11. Type category .... *category*

contin▶

Write Electronic Check (continued)

To select payee from list:

a. Click down arrow .... ⬇️

b. Click desired category.

If a check is not in Electronic Payments box:

Click **Electronic Payments** box .... `Alt` + `Y`
so a check appears.

12. Click ⬛ **Record** .... `Alt` + `C`

CLASSES

Specifies what information a transaction covers.

Create New Class

1. Click **L**ists .... `Alt` + `L`

2. Click C**l**ass .... `L`

3. Click **N**ew .... `Alt` + `N`

4. Type new class name .... *name*

5. Press **Tab** .... `Tab`

6. Type new class description .... *description*

   NOTE: The above step is optional.

7. Click [✔ **OK**] .... `↵`

Assign Class to Transaction

1. Click Acti**v**ities .... `Alt` + `V`

2. Click **W**rite Checks .... `W`

   OR

   Click Use **R**egister .... `R`

   *NOTE: When **Write Checks** is selected, you can select a Bank Account from a drop–down menu. When **Use Register** is selected, the register for the most recent account referenced is displayed.*

continu

Assign Class to Transaction (continued)

3. Enter transaction information in **Register** or **Write Checks** window.

4. Type category name .... *name* in **category** field.
   OR
   Go directly to the next step if you are not assigning a category.

5. Press **/** (slash) .... `/`

6. Type desired class .... *class*

   To select from list:

   a. Click **Lists** .... `Alt` + `L`

   b. Click **Class** .... `L`

   c. Select desired class.

   d. Click **Use** .... `Alt` + `U`

7. Click **Record** .... `Alt` + `C`

Delete Class

1. Click **Lists** .... `Alt` + `L`

2. Click **Class** .... `L`

3. Highlight class .... `↓` `↑` to delete.

4. Click **Delete** .... `Alt` + `D`

A warning message appears.

5. Click **OK** .... `↵`

Edit Class

1. Click **L**ists .... Alt + L

2. Click C**l**ass L

3. Highlight class .... ↓ ↑
   to edit.

4. Click [✍ Edit] .... Alt + I

5. Enter changes to class name, description or both.

6. Click [✔ OK] .... ↵

View Class List

1. Click **L**ists .... Alt + L

2. Click C**l**ass L

COPY FILE

NOTE: This procedure begins with opening the file you want to copy. If you are already in the file, go to step 3.

1. Click **F**ile .... Alt + F

2. Click **O**pen .... O

3. Select file to copy .... Tab , ↓ ↑
   from **File Name** list

4. Click [✔ OK] .... ↵

5. Click **F**ile .... Alt + F

6. Click **F**ile Operations .... F

continu

COPY FILE (continued)

7. Click <u>C</u>opy .... `C`

8. Type new filename................................*filename*

9. Press **Tab** .... `Tab`

10. Type new file location.............................*location*
    including directory and path.

11. Press **Tab** .... `Tab`

12. Enter beginning date .... *date*
    for transactions
    to include in new file.

13. Press **Tab** .... `Tab`

14. Enter ending date .... *date*
    for transactions
    to include in new file.

15. Press **Tab** .... `Tab`

    If you wish to exclude prior, uncleared
    transactions from new file:

    a. Click **Copy <u>A</u>ll Prior Uncleared**...... `Alt` + `A`
       Transactions to deselect.

    b. Press **Tab** .... `Tab`

    If you wish to include all prior uncleared
    transactions in new file:

    Press **Tab** .... `Tab`

continued...

86

Copy File (continued)

If you wish to exclude investment transactions from new file:

a. Click **Copy All Prior Investment....** `Alt` + `P`
Transactions to deselect.

b. Click [✔ OK] .... `↵`

If you wish to include all prior investment transactions in new file:

Click [✔ OK] .... `↵`

16. Click **Reload original copy** .... `Alt` + `R`

OR

Click **Load new copy** .... `Alt` + `L`

17. Click [✔ OK] .... `↵`

COPY REPORT TO ANOTHER PROGRAM

1. Display report as you want it copied.

2. Click [📋 Copy] .... `Alt` + `Y`

3. Switch to other program.

   NOTE: *Click in the other program's window, if visible, or press **Alt+Tab** to select the program.*

4. Position cursor where you would like data placed into other program.

5. Use other program's Paste function to copy Quicken.

   NOTE: ***Paste** is usually found in the **Edit** menu.*

CREDIT CARD TRANSACTIONS

Enter Charge into Credit Card Account

1. Click `Accts` .... `Ctrl` + `A`

The Account List appears.

2. Highlight desired account............ `Tab` , `↓` `↑`

3. Click **Open** .... `Alt` + `P`

4. Enter date.. *date*

5. Press **Tab** .... `Tab`

6. Enter reference number............................*number*

   NOTE: The above step is optional.

7 Press **Tab** .... `Tab`

8. Type payee name.. *name*

9. Press **Tab** .... `Tab`

10. Enter amount.. *amount*

11. Press **Tab** .... `Tab`

12. Type category.. *category*

13. Press **Tab** .... `Tab`

14. Type memo .... *memo*

   NOTE: The above step is optional.

15. Click **Record** .... `Alt` + `C`

Enter Credit into Credit Card Account

1. Click [Accts] .... **Alt** + **C**

The Account List appears.

2. Highlight desired account .... **Tab**, **↓** **↑**

3. Click **Open** .... **Alt** + **P**

4. Enter date .... *date*

5. Press **Tab** four times .... **Tab**, **Tab**, **Tab**, **Tab** to get to **payment** field.

6. Enter payment amount ....*amount*

7. Press **Tab** .... **Tab**

8. Type category .... *category* against which you want to apply credit.
   OR
   a. Highlight desired category from list.

   b. Press **Enter** .... **↵**

9. Type memo...*memo*
   NOTE: The above step is optional.

10. Press **Tab** .... **Tab**

11. Click [Record] .... **Alt** + **C**

CUSTOMIZE REPORT

Specifies how reports are organized and formatted, as well as what type of transfers the reports include.

Access Report Options

1. Click **Reports**..

2. Select desired **Report Family**.

3. Select desired report from list on left side of screen.

4. Click **Customize** ....

A Customize Report window appears for your chosen type of report. It will display only the options applying to the report you are creating.

5. Select desired report dates from **Report Dates** list.

   OR

   a. Click **from** box ....[Alt] + [F]
      and enter date.

   b. Click **to** box...................................[Alt] + [O]
      and enter date.

   *NOTES: At the **from** and **to** boxes, you can also access the drop–down calendar from which you can select starting and ending dates.*

   If you are customizing a Comparison report, follow step 3 for both periods of time you are going to compare.

continued...

Access Report Options (continued)

6. Choose one of the following **Customize** options:

- Report Layout .... `Alt` + `L`

- Accounts .... `Alt` + `A`

- Transactions................................. `Alt` + `N`

- Show Rows .... `Alt` + `R`

- Categories/Classes .... `Alt` + `C`

- Select to Include............................ `Alt` + `C`

- Matching .... `Alt` + `G`

7. Make appropriate changes and then select another Customize option.

8. Click [✔ OK] .... `↵`
   when finished.

EXIT QUICKEN

1. Click **File**.................................... `Alt` + `F`

2. Click **Exit**.. `X`
   If you have payments to transmit:

   Click [✔ OK] .... `↵`
   to exit anyway.
   OR
   Click **Cancel** to return to Quicken.

EXPORT TAX INFORMATION

Exports tax schedule reports and capital gains reports to other tax preparation software. To export to TurboTax for Windows, read the TurboTax for Windows User's Guide. To export to other tax preparation software, follow these steps.

1. Load Tax Schedule Report or Capital Gains Investment Report.

2. Click **Export** .... **Alt** + **X**

3 Type filename ....*filename* in **File Name** box.

4. Click **✔ OK** ....↵

   NOTE: Quicken closes the Report window and writes the data to a file that must now be accessed according to the instructions in your tax preparation software User's Guide.

FIND TRANSACTION
—IN REGISTER OR WRITE CHECKS WINDOW—

1. Click **Edit** .... **Alt** + **E**

2. Click **Find** ....**F**

3. Type word, number, phrase ....*word, number* or *phrase* matching part of transaction you want to find in appropriate field: NUM, PAYEE, MEMO, CATEGORY, PAYMENT, C (cleared status) or DEPOSIT (amount).

   NOTE: You can enter information in several of the fields. Quicken will find only those transactions meeting all specified criteria.

continued...

FIND TRANSACTION (continued)

To access additional features of Find command:

- **Search** .... Alt + S
  to tell Quicken
  which fields to search.

You can search all fields or the amount, cleared status, memo, category/class, check number or payee fields.

- **Match if** .... Alt + T
  to tell Quicken
  how to carry out the search.

You can search for transactions that start with, end with or contain a word, number or phrase you specify in the Find text box.

- Deselect **Search Backwards**.......... Alt + K
  to search from beginning
  of register if desired.

- Click [>> **Find**] .... Alt + N
  to find first/next
  matching transaction.

  OR

- Click [**Find All**] .... Alt + F
  to find all matches.

FINANCIAL CALCULATORS

*Performs **what-if calculations** to answer questions on loan refinancing and comparison as well as retirement, college and investment planning.*

College Planning Calculator

1. Click **Pl<u>a</u>n** .... `Alt` + `A`

2. Click **Financial <u>P</u>lanners** .... `P`

3. Click **<u>C</u>ollege** .... `C`

    —IN CALCULATE BOX—

    To calculate annual college costs:

    a. Click **Annual College Cos<u>t</u>s** .... `Alt` + `T`

       —IN COLLEGE INFORMATION BOX—

    b. Enter **Years <u>U</u>ntil Enrollment** .... *number*

    c. Press **Tab** .... `Tab`

    d. Enter **Number of Years <u>E</u>nrolled** .... *number* of years enrolled.

    e. Press **Tab** .... `Tab`

    f. Enter **Current College Sa<u>v</u>ings** .... *amount*

    g. Press **Tab** .... `Tab`

    h. Enter **Annual <u>Y</u>ield** percentage rate .... *rate*

    i. Press **Tab** .... `Tab`

continued...

College Planning Calculator (continued)

   j.   Enter **Annual Contribution** ....*amount*

   k. Press **Tab** .... `Tab`

   l. Enter **Predicted Inflation** rate......................*rate*

To adjust contributions by predicted inflation rate:

Click **Inflate Contributions** .... `Alt` + `F`

If you do not want to adjust annual contributions for predicted inflation:

Leave as is.

To show deposit schedule:

Click [🖳 **Schedule...**] .... `Alt` + `S`

To calculate current savings required:

       —*IN CALCULATE BOX*—

   a. Click **Current College Savings** .... `Alt` + `G`

     —*IN COLLEGE INFORMATION BOX*—

   b. Enter **Annual College Costs** ....*amount*

   c. Press **Tab** .... `Tab`

   d. Enter **Years Until Enrollment** .... *number*

   e. Press **Tab** .... `Tab`

   f. Enter **Number of Years Enrolled** .... *number*

   g. Press **Tab** .... `Tab`

contin

College Planning Calculator (continued)

h. Enter **Annual Yield** percentage rate .... *rate*

i. Press **Tab** .... `Tab`

j. Enter **Annual Contribution** .... *amount*

k. Press **Tab** .... `Tab`

l. Enter **Predicted Inflation** rate .... *rate*

To adjust contributions by predicted inflation rate:

Click **Inflate Contributions** .... `Alt` + `F`

If you do not want to adjust annual contributions for predicted inflation:

Leave as is.

To show deposit schedule:

Click **Schedule** .... `Alt` + `S`

To calculate Annual Contribution required:

—IN CALCULATE BOX—

a. Click **Annual Contribution** .... `Alt` + `B`

—IN COLLEGE INFORMATION BOX—

b. Enter **Annual College Costs** .... *amount*

c. Press **Tab** .... `Tab`

d. Enter **Years Until Enrollment** .... *number*

e. Press **Tab** .... `Tab`

continued...

College Planning Calculator (continued)

f. Enter **Number of Years Enrolled** .... *number*

g. Press **Tab** .... `Tab`

h. Enter **Current College Savings** ....*amount*

i. Press **Tab** .... `Tab`

j. Enter **Annual Yield** percentage rate ....*rate*

k. Press **Tab** .... `Tab`

l. Enter **Predicted Inflation** rate ....*rate*

To adjust contributions by predicted inflation rate:

Click **Inflate Contributions** .... `Alt` + `F`

If you do not want to adjust annual contributions for predicted inflation:

Leave as is.

To show deposit schedule:

Click **Schedule** .... `Alt` + `S`

Loan Calculator

1. Click **Pla̲n** .... [Alt] + [A]

2. Click **Financial P̲lanners** .... [P]

3. Click **L̲oan** .... [L]

    To calculate loan amount (you can afford to borrow given a particular payment plan)**:**

    —IN CALCULATE BOX—

    a. Click **Loan A̲mount** .... [Alt] + [A]

    b. Enter **Annual I̲nterest Rate** .... *rate*

    c. Press **Tab** .... [Tab]

    d. Enter **Number of Y̲ears** .... *number* loan covers.

    e. Press **Tab** .... [Tab]

    f. Enter **Pe̲riods Per Year** .... *number* of payments per year.

    g. Press **Tab** .... [Tab]

    h. Enter **P̲ayment Per Period** .... *amount*

    i. Press **Tab** .... [Tab]

To view payment schedule:

Click [⎙ S̲chedule...] .... [Alt] + [S]

continued...

Loan Calculator (continued)

To calculate regular payments required:

—IN CALCULATE BOX—

a. Click **Payment Per Period** .... Alt + T

—IN LOAN INFORMATION BOX—

b. Enter **Loan Amount**.................................*amount*

c. Press **Tab** .... Tab

d. Enter **Annual Interest Rate**..........................*rate*

e. Press **Tab** .... Tab

f. Enter **Number of Years**........................ *number* loan covers.

g. Press **Tab** .... Tab

h. Enter **Periods Per Year**........................ *number* of payments per year.

i. Press **Tab** .... Tab

To view payment schedule:

Click Schedule... .... Alt + S

Retirement Planning Calculator

1. Click **Plan** .... `Alt` + `A`

2. Click **Financial Planners** .... `F`

3. Click **Retirement** .... `R`

   To calculate current savings required:

   —IN RETIREMENT INFORMATION BOX—

   a. Click **Current Savings** .... `Alt` + `G`

   —IN RETIREMENT INFORMATION BOX—

   b. Enter **Annual Yield** .... *yield*

   c. Press **Tab** .... `Tab`

   d. Enter **Annual Contribution** .... *amount*

   e. Press **Tab** .... `Tab`

   f. Enter **Current Age** .... *number*

   g. Press **Tab** .... `Tab`

   h. Enter **Retirement Age** .... *number*

   i. Press **Tab** .... `Tab`

   j. Enter **Withdraw Until Age** .... *number*

   k. Press **Tab** .... `Tab`

   l. Enter **Other Income** .... *amount*

   m. Press **Tab** .... `Tab`

continued...

100

Retirement Planning Calculator (continued)

n. Enter **Annual Retirement Income** ....*amount* **After Taxes**.

o. Press **Tab** .... `Tab`

—IN TAX INFORMATION BOX—

If savings are tax-sheltered:

Click **Tax-sheltered Investment**.... `Alt` + `X`

If savings are not tax-sheltered:

Click **Non–Sheltered Investment**.. `Alt` + `L`

p. Press **Tab** .... `Tab`

q. Enter **Current Tax Rate**...................*rate*

r. Press **Tab** .... `Tab`

s. Enter **Retirement Tax Rate** ....*rate*

t. Press **Tab** .... `Tab`

—IN INFLATION BOX—

u. Enter **Predicted Inflation** rate......................*rate*

v. Press **Tab** .... `Tab`

To adjust contributions for inflation:

Click **Inflate Contributions** .... `Alt` + `F`

If you want annual income in today's dollars:

Click **Annual Income in Today's $**....... `Alt` + `T`

continu

Retirement Planning Calculator (continued)

To view payment schedule:

Click [📇 Schedule...] .... `Alt` + `S`

To calculate annual contribution required:

—IN CALCULATE BOX—

a. Click Annual Contri**b**ution .... `Alt` + `B`

—IN RETIREMENT INFORMATION BOX—

b. Enter **Current Savings** .... *amount*

c. Press **Tab** .... `Tab`

d. Enter **Annual Yield** .... *yield*

e. Press **Tab** .... `Tab`

f. Enter **Current Age** .... *number*

g. Press **Tab** .... `Tab`

h. Enter **Retirement Age** .... *number*

i. Press **Tab** .... `Tab`

j. Enter **Withdraw Until Age** .... *number*

k. Press **Tab** .... `Tab`

l. Enter **Other Income** .... *amount*

m. Press **Tab** .... `Tab`

n. Enter **Annual Retirement Income** .... *amount*
   After Taxes.

continued...

Retirement Planning Calculator (continued)

o. Press **Tab** .... Tab

   If savings are tax-sheltered:

   Click **Tax-sheltered Investment**.... Alt + X

   If savings are not tax-sheltered:

   Click **Non–Sheltered Investment** .. Alt + L

p. Press **Tab** .... Tab

q. Enter **Current Tax Rate** .... *rate*

r. Press **Tab** .... Tab

s. Enter **Retirement Tax Rate** .... *rate*

t. Press **Tab** .... Tab

u. Enter **Predicted Inflation** rate .... *rate*

v. Press **Tab** .... Tab

To adjust contributions for inflation:

Click **Inflate Contributions** .... Alt + F

If you want annual income in today's dollars:

Click **Annual Income in Today's $** .... Alt + T

To view payment schedule:

Click [📠 **Schedule...**] .... Alt + S

continu

Retirement Planning Calculator (continued)

To calculate annual retirement income:
>   —*IN CALCULATE BOX*—

a. Click **Annual Retirement Income**.... `Alt` + `O`
>   —*IN RETIREMENT INFORMATION BOX*—

b. Enter **Current Savings**............................ *amount*

c. Press **Tab** .... `Tab`

d. Enter **Annual Yield** ....*yield*

e. Press **Tab** .... `Tab`

f. Enter **Annual Contribution** .... *amount*

g. Press **Tab** .... `Tab`

h. Enter **Current Age** ....*number*

i. Press **Tab** .... `Tab`

j. Enter **Retirement Age** ....*number*

k. Press **Tab** .... `Tab`

l. Enter **Withdraw Until Age** ....*number*

m. Press **Tab** .... `Tab`

n. Enter **Other Income**............................... *amount*

o. Press **Tab** .... `Tab`

   If savings are tax-sheltered:

   Click **Tax-sheltered Investment**...... `Alt` + `X`

   If savings are not tax-sheltered:

continued...

Retirement Planning Calculator (continued)

Click **Non–She̲ltered Investment**.... Alt + L

p. Press **Tab** .... Tab

q. Enter **Curre̲nt Tax Rate**............................... *rate*

r. Press **Tab** .... Tab

s. Enter **Retire̲ment Tax Rate** .... *rate*

t. Press **Tab** .... Tab

u. Enter **Predicted I̲nflation** rate..................... *rate*

v. Press **Tab** .... Tab

To adjust contributions for inflation:

Click **Inf̲late Contributions** .... Alt + F

If you want annual income in today's dollars:

Click **Annual Income in T̲oday's $** ...... Alt + T

To view payment schedule:

Click Schedule... .... Alt + S

SAVINGS CALCULATOR

1. Click **Pl_a_n** .... `Alt` + `A`

2. Click **Financial _P_lanners** .... `P`

3. Click **_S_avings** .... `S`

—IN CALCULATE BOX—

To calculate opening savings balance required:

a. Click **Opening Sa_v_ings Balance** ..... `Alt` + `V`

—IN SAVINGS INFORMATION BOX—

b. Enter **Annual _Y_ield** .... *yield*

c. Press **Tab** twice .... `Tab`
   to move to **_N_umber of** box.

   To select period other than yearly:

   i. Click down arrow .... `↓`

   ii. Choose option from list.

   iii. Press **Tab** .... `Tab`

d. Enter number .... *number*
   of years, weeks, months or quarters.

e. Press **Tab** .... `Tab`
   to move to **Contributions Each** box.

   To have contributions based on period other than yearly:

   i. Click down arrow .... `↓`

continued...

106

Savings Calculator (continued)

    ii. Choose option from list.

    iii. Press **Tab**.. `Tab`

f. Enter amount ....*amount*
   of periodic contribution.

g. Press **Tab** .... `Tab`

h. Enter desired ending savings balance ....*amount*

i. Press **Tab** .... `Tab`

    —IN INFLATION BOX—

j. Enter **Predicted Inflation Rate** ....*rate*

k. Press **Tab** .... `Tab`

To adjust contributions for inflation:

Click **Inflate Contributions** .... `Alt` + `F`

If you want ending balance in today's dollars:

Click **Ending Balance in Today's $** ...... `Alt` + `T`

To view payment schedule:

Click [📋 Schedule...] .... `Alt` + `S`

To calculate regular contributions required:

    —IN SAVINGS INFORMATION BOX—

a. Click **Regular Contribution** .... `Alt` + `R`

continue

Savings Calculator (continued)

—IN SAVINGS INFORMATION BOX—

b. Enter **Opening Savings Balance** .... *amount*

c. Press **Tab** .... `Tab`

d. Enter **Annual Yield** .... *yield*

e. Press **Tab** .... `Tab`

To select period other than yearly:

i. Click down arrow.

ii. Choose option from list.

iii. Press **Tab** .... `Tab`

f. Enter number .... *number*
of years, weeks,
months or quarters.

g. Press **Tab** .... `Tab`

To have contributions based on a period other than yearly:

i. Click down arrow.

ii. Choose option from list.

iii. Press **Tab** .... `Tab`

h. Enter desired **Ending Savings Balance** . *amount*

i. Press **Tab** .... `Tab`

j. Enter **Predicted Inflation Rate** .... *rate*

continued...

108

Savings Calculator (continued)

k. Press **Tab** .... `Tab`

To adjust contributions for inflation:

Click **Inflate Contributions** .... `Alt` + `F`

If you want ending balance in today's dollars:

Click **Ending Balance in Today's $** ...... `Alt` + `T`

To view payment schedule:

Click `Schedule...` .... `Alt` + `S`

To calculate ending savings balance:

a. Click **Ending Savings Balance** .... `Alt` + `B`

b. Enter **Opening Savings Balance** ....*amount*

c. Press **Tab** .... `Tab`

d. Enter **Annual Yield** .... *yield*

e. Press **Tab** .... `Tab`

   To select period other than yearly:

   i. Click down arrow .... `↓`

   ii. Choose option from list.

   iii. Press **Tab** .... `Tab`

f. Enter number.................................... *number*
   of years, weeks,
   months or quarters.

g. Press **Tab** .... `Tab`

continu

Savings Calculator (continued)

To have contributions based on period other than yearly:

i. Click down arrow .... ⬇️

ii. Choose option from list.

iii. Press **Tab** .... Tab

h. Enter amount .... *amount* of periodic contribution.

i. Press **Tab** .... Tab

j. Enter **Predicted Inflation Rate** .... *rate*

k. Press **Tab** .... Tab

To adjust contributions for inflation:

Click **Inflate Contributions** .... Alt + F

If you want ending balance in today's dollars:

Click **Ending Balance in Today's $** ...... Alt + T

To view payment schedule:

Click [Schedule...] .... Alt + S

FINANCIAL CALENDAR

View Calendar

1. Click [Calendar] .... [Ctrl] + [K]

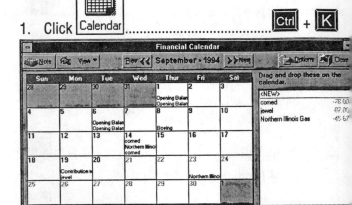

—IN FINANCIAL CALENDAR WINDOW—

To schedule a transaction on the calendar:

a. Select desired month.

- Click [Prev **<<**] .... [Alt] + [P]

- Click [**>>** Next] .... [Alt] + [T]

b. Point to desired transaction.

  Mouse pointer changes to hand.

c. Click, hold and drag transaction to date.

   OR

   i. Click <NEW> and drag to date.

   ii. Enter information in **Drag and Drop Transaction** window.

continu■

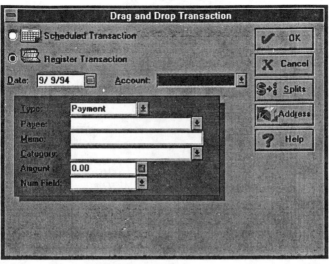

iii. Click [✔ OK] .... ↵

To add note to calendar:

a. Click desired date .... ↓ ↑ → ←

b. Click [Note] .... Alt + N

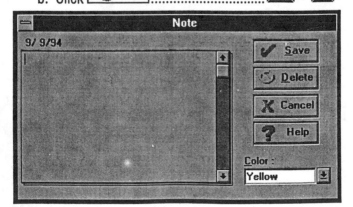

continued...

112

View Calendar (continued)

    c. Type note..*note*

    d. Click **✔ Save**............................... `Alt` + `S`

2. Click **✈ Close** to exit calendar.

FORECAST

1. Click **Plan**...................................... `Alt` + `A`, `F`

    —IN AUTOMATICALLY CREATE
    FORECAST WINDOW—

2. Change **Date Range to Read**, if desired.

   To customize the forecast:

    a. Click **🏠 Advanced...**

    b. Select desired options from the following:

      To select accounts:

      i. Click **📧 Accounts...** .... `Alt` + `A`

      ii. Select desired options.

      iii. Click **✔ OK** .... `↵`

      To select categories:

      i. Click **📧 Categories...** .... `Alt` + `C`

      ii. Select desired options.

      iii. Click **✔ OK** .... `↵`

3. Click **✔ Done** .... `Alt` + `D`

continu

4. Click [✔ **OK**] ....[↵]
   to view forecast.

   —IN FORECASTING BASE SCENARIO WINDOW—

5. Make desired adjustments to base scenario:

   - Click [🖳 S̲cenario] .... [Alt] + [S]
     to change amounts or compare
     different possibilities.

   - Click [📇Acco̲unts] .... [Alt] + [U]
     to select desired account balances.

   - Click [🔧 C̲reate] .... [Alt] + [C]
     to create forecast from data
     already entered.

   - Click [🔢 T̲rack] .... [Alt] + [T]
     estimatcd items in forecast.

6. Click [🚪 Close] when finished.

GRAPHS

Create Income and Expense Graphs

1. Click [Graphs]

   OR

   a. Click **Reports** menu .... `Alt` + `R`

   b. Click **Graphs** .... `G`

   c. Click **Income and Expense** .... `I`

2. Click **Income and Expense Graph** .... `Alt` + `I`

3. Click **From** box................................... `Alt` + `F`
   and enter date.

4. Click **To** box...................................... `Alt` + `T`
   and enter date.

   If you want to include subcategories:

   Click **Show subcategories in graph** ..... `Alt` + `S`

5. Click **Accounts** .... `Alt` + `A`

   —AT SELECT ACCOUNTS TO INCLUDE BOX—

   If desired account is selected:

   Click next desired account, or go to step 6.

continu

Create Income and Expense Graphs (continued)

If desired account is not marked to include:

Click desired account.

*A check mark (✔) appears in column to left of **Account** list.*

To select all accounts:

Click | **Mark All** |........................| Alt | + | A |

> NOTE: *To exclude marked accounts, click account*
> *to remove check mark.*

6. Click | ✔ **OK** |..| ↵ |

7. Click **Categories**...............................| Alt | + | C |

——*IN SELECT CATEGORIES TO INCLUDE BOX*——

If desired category is marked to include:

Click next desired category, or go to step 8.

If desired category is not marked to include:

Click desired category.

*A check mark (✔) appears in column to left of **Category** list.*

To select all categories:

Click | **Mark All** |........................| Alt | + | A |

> NOTE: *To exclude marked accounts, click account*
> *to remove check mark.*

8. Click | ✔ **OK** |..| ↵ |

9. Click **Classes**...................................| Alt | + | L |

continued...

Create Income and Expense Graphs (continued)

—IN SELECT CLASSES TO INCLUDE BOX—

If desired class is selected:

Click next desired class, or go to step 10.

If desired class is not selected:

Click desired class.

*A check mark (✔) appears in column to left of **Class** list.*

To select all classes:

Click **🐾 Mark All** .... **Alt** + **A**

NOTE: To exclude marked accounts, click account
to remove check mark.

10. Click **✔ OK** .... **↵**

11. Click **Create** .... **Alt** + **R**

Create Budget Variance Graphs

1. Click **Graphs**

   OR

   a. Click **Reports** menu .... **Alt** + **R**

   b. Click **Graphs** .... **G**

   c. Click **Budget Variance** .... **B**

2. Click **Budget Variance Graph** .... **Alt** + **B**

continu

117

Create Budget Variance Graphs (continued)

3. Click **From** box .... `Alt` + `F`
   and enter date.

4. Click **To** box.................................... `Alt` + `T`
   and enter date.

   To include subcategories:

   Click **Show subcategories in graph** .... `S`

5. Click **Accounts**............................... `Alt` + `A`

   —IN SELECT ACCOUNTS TO INCLUDE BOX—

   If desired account is selected:

   Click next desired account, or go to step 6.

   If desired account is not selected:

   Click desired account.

A check mark (✔) appears in column to left of Account list.

   To select all accounts:

   Click [✿ **Mark All**] .... `Alt` + `A`

   *NOTE: To exclude marked accounts, click account
   to remove check mark.*

6. Click [✔ **OK**] .... `↵`

7. Click **Categories**............................. `Alt` + `C`

continued...

Create Budget Variance Graphs (continued)

—IN SELECT CATEGORIES TO INCLUDE BOX—

If desired category is selected:

Click next desired category, or go to step 8.

If desired category is not selected:

Click desired category.

A check mark (✔) appears in column to left of Category list.

To select all categories:

Click [✔✔✔ **M**ark All] .... [Alt] + [A]

> *NOTE:* To exclude marked accounts, click account
> to remove check mark.

8. Click [✔ OK] .... [↵]

9. Click C**l**asses .... [Alt] + [L]

—IN SELECT CLASSES TO INCLUDE BOX—

If desired class is selected:

Click next desired class, or go to step 10.

If desired class is not selected:

Click desired class.

A check mark (✔) appears in column to left of Class list.

To select all classes:

Click [✔✔✔ **M**ark All] .... [Alt] + [A]

> *NOTE:* To exclude marked accounts, click account
> to remove check mark.

10. Click [✔ OK] .... [↵]

11. Click C**r**eate .... [Alt] + [R]

Create Net Worth Graphs

1. Click Graphs

   OR

   a. Click **R**eports menu........................ Alt + R

   b. Click **G**raphs................................... G

   c. Click **N**et Worth.............................. N

2. Click **N**et Worth Graph..................... Alt + N

3. Click **F**rom box................................. Alt + F
   and enter date.

4. Click **T**o box.................................... Alt + T
   and enter date.

5. Press **Tab**....................................... Tab

6. Click **A**ccounts................................ Alt + A

   —IN SELECT ACCOUNTS TO INCLUDE BOX—

   If desired account is selected:

   Click next desired account, or go to step 6.

   If desired account is not marked Include:

   Click desired account.

A check mark (✔) appears in column to left of Account list.

continued...

Create Net Worth Graphs (continued)

To select all accounts:

Click [***Mark All***] .... `Alt` + `A`

*NOTE: To exclude marked accounts, click account
to remove check mark.*

7. Click [✔ **OK**] .... `⏎`

8. Click **C**ategories .... `Alt` + `C`

——*IN SELECT CATEGORIES TO INCLUDE BOX*—

If desired category is selected:

Click next desired category, or go to step 8.

If desired category is not selected:

Click desired category.

*A check mark (✔) appears in column to left of **Category** list.*

To select all categories:

Click [***Mark All***] .... `Alt` + `A`

*NOTE: To exclude marked accounts, click account
to remove check mark.*

9. Click [✔ **OK**] .... `⏎`

10. Click C**l**asses .... `Alt` + `L`

—*IN SELECT CLASSES TO INCLUDE BOX*—

If desired class is marked to include:

Click next desired class, or go to step 10.

continu

Create Net Worth Graphs (continued)

If desired class is not selected:

Click desired class.

*A check mark (✔) appears in column to left of **Class** list.*

To select all class:

Click ▨▨ **Mark All** .... Alt + A

> *NOTE:* To exclude marked accounts, click account
> to remove check mark.

11. Click ✔ **OK** .... ↵

12. Click C**r**eate .... Alt + R

Create Investment Graphs

1. Click [Graphs]

    OR

    a. Click **R**eports menu .... Alt + R

    b. Click **G**raphs .... G

    c. Click In**v**estment V

2. Click In**v**estment Graph .... Alt + V

3. Click **F**rom box .... Alt + F
   and enter date.

4. Click **T**o box .... Alt + T
   and enter date.

continued...

Create Investment Graphs (continued)

5. Click <u>A</u>ccounts .... `Alt` + `A`

    —IN SELECT ACCOUNTS TO INCLUDE BOX—

    If desired account is selected:

    Click next desired account, or go to step 6.

    If desired account is not selected:

    Click desired account.

    *A check mark (✔) appears in column to left of **Account** list.*

    To select all accounts:

    Click | ✔✔✔ **M**ark All | .... `Alt` + `A`

    *NOTE: To exclude marked accounts, click account
    to remove check mark.*

6. Click | ✔ OK | .... `↵`

7. Click <u>S</u>ecurities .... `Alt` + `S`

    —IN SELECT SECURITIES TO INCLUDE BOX—

    If desired security is selected:

    Click next desired security, or go to step 8.

    If desired security is not selected:

    Click desired security.

    *A check mark (✔) appears in column to left of **Security** list.*

    To select all securities:

    Click | ✔✔✔ **M**ark All | .... `Alt` + `A`

    *NOTE: To exclude marked accounts, click account
    to remove check mark.*

8. Click | ✔ OK | .... `↵`

9. Click C<u>r</u>eate .... `Alt` + `R`

HELP

*Help is accessed from anywhere within Quicken by pressing **F1** or the **Help** icon.*

Context-Sensitive Help

Gives help on the current screen, window or menu.

1. Click 🛐Help F1

2. Use up and down arrow keys .... ↑ ↓

   OR

   Press **PgUp** or **PgDn** .... Page Up or Page Down
   to scroll through **Help**
   messages too long
   to fit on one screen.

   OR

   Use mouse to scroll through **Help** messages.

Copy Help Information

*Copies **Help** information to the clipboard.*

1. Click 🛐Help F1

2. Click **E**dit .... Alt + E

3. Click **C**opy C

4. Click and drag over text to copy.

5. Click **C**opy .... Alt + C

6. Copy contents of clipboard to desired location.

Annotate Help Topics

*Annotates the current **Help** topic for future reference.*

1. Click [Help icon] .... `F1`

2. Click **E**dit... `Alt` + `E`

3. Click **A**nnotate .... `A`

4. Type annotation ....*note*
   in **A**nnotation dialog box.

5. Click **S**ave... `Alt` + `S`

   *NOTE: A **paper clip** appears next to the annotated*
   ***Help** topic title.*

   To review annotation:

   —FROM ANNOTATED HELP TOPIC—

   Click paper clip.

Mark Help Topics for Easy Access

—FROM HELP TOPIC TO MARK—

1. Click [Help icon] .... `F1`

2. Click **Book**m**ark**............................... `Alt` + `M`

3. Click **D**efine .... `D`

   To use name in **Bookmark Name text box:**

   Click **OK** .... ✔ OK

continu

Mark Help Topics for Easy Access (continued)

To use a different name:

a. Type new name................................ *name*
   in **Bookmark Name** text box.

b. Click [✔ OK] .... [↵]

To access marked Help entries:

Click [? Help] .... [F1]

4. Click **Bookmark** .... [Alt] + [M]

5. Click desired topic name.

Help Search

1. Click [? Help] .... [F1]

2. Click **Search** .... [S]

3. Type topic.................................... *topic*
   for which you
   want to search.

   OR

   Select topic from scroll box.

4. Click **Show Topics** .... [S]

5. Select topic in bottom field.

6. Click **Go To** .... [Alt] + [G]

126

Help Print

*Prints current **Help** topic.*

1. Click [Help] .... `F1`

2. Click **P**rint .... `P`

ICONBAR

Lets you access Quicken's most commonly used menu items by clicking the desired icon on the iconbar.

Customize Iconbar

Lets you change the appearance of the iconbar. You can choose which graphics represent each icon command and whether or not the icons displayed contain graphics, text or both. You can also reset Quicken's default iconbar.

Add New Icon to Iconbar

1. Click [Options] .... `Alt` + `E`, `O`

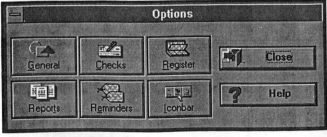

2. Click [Iconbar] .... `Alt` + `I`

continu

Add New Icon to Iconbar (continued)

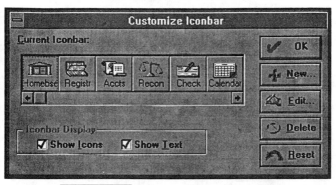

3. Click  [Alt] + [N]

4. Select action to add from **Icon Action** scroll box.

The default graphic for the action appears to the right of the scroll box.

5. Click [✔ OK] twice .... [↵], [↵]

6. Click [✔ Done] .... [Alt] + [D]

Delete Icon from Iconbar

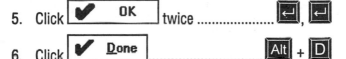

1. Click [Options] .... [Alt] + [E], [O]

2. Click [Iconbar] .... [Alt] + [I]

3. Select icon to delete from **Current Iconbar** scroll box.

continued...

Delete Icon from Iconbar (continued)

4. Click | 🚫 D̲elete | .... Alt + D

A warning window appears.

5. Click | ✔ OK | twice .... ↵ , ↵

6. Click | ➡️ C̲lose |

Change Icon Graphic

1. Click | Options | .... Alt + E , O

2. Click | I̲conbar | .... Alt + I

3. Click | 🖐 Ed̲it | .... Alt + E

   OR

   Click | ➕ N̲ew | .... Alt + N

4. Select action to change from **Icon A̲ction** box.

The default graphic for the action appears to the right of the scroll box.

5. Click | 🖐 Change | .... Alt + E
   in **Edit Action on Iconbar** window.

6. Select desired graphic from **G̲raphic** scroll box.

7. Click | ✔ OK | three times ... ↵ , ↵ , ↵

8. Click | ➡️ C̲lose | .... ↵

Change Icon Text

1. Click Options .... Alt + E , O

2. Click Iconbar .... Alt + I

3. Click Edit .... Alt + E

   OR

   Click New .... Alt + N

4. Select action to change from **Icon Action** box.

The default graphic for the action appears to the right of the scroll box.

5. Click Change .... Alt + E
   in **Edit Action on Iconbar** window.

6. Click **Icon Text** box...................... Alt + I

7. Type desired text.. *text*
   in **Icon Text** box.

8. Click OK three times... ↵ , ↵ , ↵

9. Click Close .... ↵

130

Reset Default Iconbar

1. Click [Options] .... `Alt` + `E` , `O`

2. Click [Iconbar] .... `Alt` + `I`

3. Click [Reset] .... `Alt` + `R`

A warning window appears.

4. Click [OK] twice .... `⏎` `⏎`

> NOTE: If you have installed this version of
> Quicken for Windows over a previous
> version, and if you have customized your
> previous iconbar, the settings you chose
> then may be automatically retained by the
> new version of Quicken. If you wish, you
> can upgrade your iconbar to the Quicken 4
> for Windows iconbar by resetting the
> default iconbar.

5. Click [Close] .... `⏎`

Show Only Icon Graphics

1. Click [Options] .... `Alt` + `E` , `O`

2. Click [Iconbar] .... `Alt` + `I`

contin

Show Only Icon Graphics (continued)

3. Deselect **Show T̲ext** box .... `Alt` + `T`

Text will not appear on iconbar.

> NOTE: To restore text, select **Show Text** box.

4. Click ✔ OK .... `↵`

5. Click ➡ **Close** .... `↵`

Show Only Icon Text

1. Click [Options] .... `Alt` + `E`, `O`

2. Click [Iconbar] .... `Alt` + `I`

3. Deselect **Show I̲cons** box .... `Alt` + `I`

Graphics will not appear on iconbar.

> NOTE: To restore graphics, select **Show Icons** box.

4. Click ✔ OK .... `↵`

5. Click ➡ **Close** .... `↵`

Rearrange Iconbar

Click and drag icon to new position on iconbar.

The other icons will shift to the left or right to accommodate the new position of the icon.

INTELLICHARGE

IntelliCharge is Quicken's electronic credit card payment system. To use this feature you must have a Quicken credit card. (See your Quicken User's Guide for more information.)

Set Up IntelliCharge Account

1. Click **Acti̲vities** .... `Alt` + `V`

2. Click **Create N̲ew Account** .... `N`

3. Click **Cr̲edit Card Account** .... `Alt` + `R`

   Click **A̲ccount Name** .... `Alt` + `A`
   and type name.

   Click **B̲alance** .... `Alt` + `B`
   and enter amount.

   Click **as̲ of** .... `Alt` + `S`
   and enter date.

   Click **Enable In̲telliCharge** .... `Alt` + `N`
   to select.

   —IN OPTIONAL INFORMATION BOX—

   Click **C̲redit Card Number** .... `Alt` + `C`
   and enter number.

   Click **Credit L̲imit** .... `Alt` + `L`
   and enter amount.

continue

Set Up IntelliCharge Account (continued)

If you receive your statement via modem:

a. Select statement delivery:

- Dis**k**ette
- **M**odem

b. Click **Social Security Number** .... `Alt` + `S`
   and enter number.

c. Click **IntelliCharge Password** .... `Alt` + `P`
   and enter password.

d. Click [✔ **Done**] .... `↵`

continued...

Set Up IntelliCharge Account (continued)

If you receive your statement via disk:

a. Click **Diskette** .... `Alt` + `K`

b. Click [✔ **Done**] .... `↵`

NOTE: *The account is set up, but you still have to*
set up your modem.

You are now in the register for the new account from which you
can exit.

Update IntelliCharge Accounts

1. Click [🗒 Accts]

The Account List appears.

2. Highlight desired IntelliCharge account .... `↓` `↑`

3. Click **Activities** .... `Alt` + `V`

4. Click **Get IntelliCharge Data** .... `C`

If you receive IntelliCharge data via modem:

a. Make sure your modem is set up correctly.

b. Click [✔ **OK**] .... `↵`
   to download data.

If you receive IntelliCharge data via disk:

a. Insert IntelliCharge statement disk in floppy
   drive.

b. Enter floppy drive letter ....*letter*

c. Click [✔ **OK**] .... `↵`

INVESTMENT ACCOUNTS

Keeps track of investments in stocks, bonds, mutual funds and other securities fluctuating in price.

1. Click **L**ists .... `Alt` + `L`

2. Click **S**ecurity .... `S`

3. Click **Acti**v**ities** .... `Alt` + `V`

4. Click **Create** **N**ew **Account** .... `N`

5. Click **I**nvestment .... `Alt` + `I`

6. Type **A**ccount **Name** .... *name*

   Click **Tax–Deferred Account**

   IRA, 401(k), etc. .... `Alt` + `T`
   if account is tax deferred.

   If account is a single mutual fund:

   a. Click **Account Contains a Single** ..... `Alt` + `M`
      Mutual Fund.

   b. Click **D**escription box .... `Alt` + `D`

   c. Type account description .... *description*

   d. Click [✔ **OK**] .... `↵`

continued...

Investment Accounts (continued)

If account contains a single Mutual Fund, the Set Up Mutual Fund Security window appears.

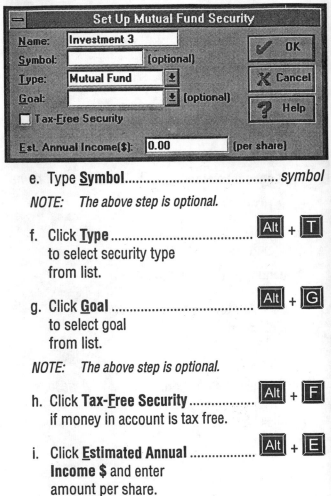

e. Type **Symbol**.. *symbol*

NOTE: The above step is optional.

f. Click **Type** .... Alt + T
   to select security type
   from list.

g. Click **Goal** .... Alt + G
   to select goal
   from list.

NOTE: The above step is optional.

h. Click **Tax-Free Security** .... Alt + F
   if money in account is tax free.

i. Click **Estimated Annual** .... Alt + E
   Income $ and enter
   amount per share.

continu

Investment Accounts (continued)

j. Click **✔ OK** .... ⏎

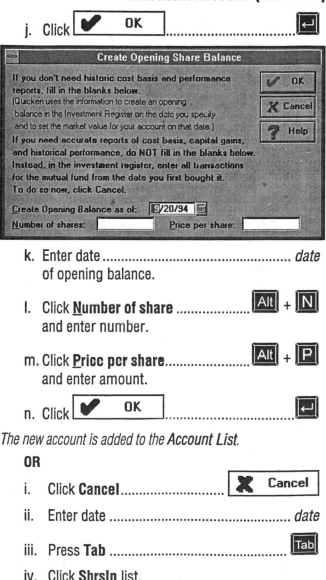

Create Opening Share Balance

If you don't need historic cost basis and performance reports, fill in the blanks below.
[Quicken uses the information to create an opening balance in the Investment Register on the date you specify and to set the market value for your account on that date.]

If you need accurate reports of cost basis, capital gains, and historical performance, do NOT fill in the blanks below. Instead, in the investment register, enter all transactions for the mutual fund from the date you first bought it.
To do so now, click Cancel.

✔ OK

✗ Cancel

? Help

Create Opening Balance as of: **9/20/94**
Number of shares: _____   Price per share: _____

k. Enter date .... *date*
of opening balance.

l. Click **Number of share** .... **Alt** + **N**
and enter number.

m. Click **Price per share** .... **Alt** + **P**
and enter amount.

n. Click **✔ OK** .... ⏎

*The new account is added to the **Account List**.*

OR

i. Click **Cancel** .... **✗ Cancel**

ii. Enter date .... *date*

iii. Press **Tab** .... **Tab**

iv. Click **ShrsIn** list.

continued...

Investment Accounts (continued)

v. Press **Tab** .... `Tab`

vi. Enter price per share .... *amount*

vii. Press **Tab** .... `Tab`

viii. Enter number of shares .... *number*

ix. Click **Record** .... `Alt` + `C`

NOTE: *If the number in the shares field is incorrect, click **Update Balances** from the **Activities** menu. Then, click **Update Share Balance**.*

If account is not a single mutual fund:

a. Click **Description** box .... `Alt` + `T`

b. Type account description .... *description*

c. Click ✔ **OK** twice .... `↵`, `↵`

Edit Name and/or Description of Investment Account

1. Click **Accts**

2. Highlight investment account .... `↓` `↑` to edit.

3. Click **Edit** .... `Alt` + `I`

4. Make desired changes.

5. Click ✔ **OK** .... `↵`

Delete Investment Account

1. Click **Accts**

2. Highlight investment account .... ↓ ↑
   to delete.

3. Click 🚫 **Delete** .... Alt + D

4. Type *yes* .... Y E S
   to confirm deletion.

5. Click ✔ **OK** .... ↵

Adjust Share Balance in Investment Account

1. Click **Accts**

2. Highlight investment account .... ↓ ↑
   to delete.

3. Click **Open** .... Alt + P

4. Click **Activities** .... Alt + V

5. Click **Update Balances** .... U

6. Click **Update Shares Balance** .... S

7. Enter adjustment date .... *date*

8. Click **Number of shares** .... Alt + N
   and enter number of shares.

9. Click ✔ **OK** .... ↵

INVESTMENT GOALS

Add New Investment Goal

1. Click **Lists** .... `Alt` + `L`

2. Click **Investment Goal** .... `O`

3. Click **New** .... `Alt` + `N`

4. Enter **Goal** name .... *name*

5. Click [✔ **OK**] .... `↵`

Delete Investment Goal

1. Click **Lists** .... `Alt` + `L`

2. Click **Investment Goal** .... `O`

3. Highlight investment account .... `↓` `↑`

4. Click [🚫 **Delete**] .... `Alt` + `D`

5. Click [✔ **OK**] .... `↵`

Edit Investment Goal

1. Click **Lists** .... `Alt` + `L`

2. Click **Investment Goal** .... `O`

3. Highlight investment account .... `↓` `↑`

4. Click **Edit** .... `Alt` + `I`

5. Type new **Goal** name .... *name*

6. Click [✔ **OK**] .... `↵`

INVESTMENT INCOME REPORT

1. Click <kbd>Reports</kbd>

2. Click **Investment** .... <kbd>Alt</kbd> + <kbd>I</kbd>

3. Click **Investment Income** .... <kbd>Tab</kbd>, <kbd>↓</kbd> <kbd>↑</kbd>

4. Click <kbd>Customize</kbd> .... <kbd>Alt</kbd> + <kbd>C</kbd>

5. Select desired report dates........................ <kbd>↓</kbd> <kbd>↑</kbd>
   from **Report Dates** list.

   OR

   a. Click **from** box .... <kbd>Alt</kbd> + <kbd>F</kbd>
      and enter date.

   b. Click **to** box.................................. <kbd>Alt</kbd> + <kbd>O</kbd>
      and enter date.

   NOTE: *At the **from** and **to** boxes, you can also*
   access the drop-down calendar from which
   you can select starting and ending dates.

6. Click **Title** box .... <kbd>Alt</kbd> + <kbd>I</kbd>

7. Type report title .... *title*

8. Click **Subtotal By** box .... <kbd>Alt</kbd> + <kbd>U</kbd>

9. Select subtotal option................................ <kbd>↓</kbd> <kbd>↑</kbd>
   from list.

Investment Income Report (continued)

10. Click **Organization** box .... Alt + Z

11. Choose one of the following **Organization** options:

    - Income and Expense

    - Cash flow basis

    If you want amounts rounded to nearest dollar:

    Deselect **Show Cents in Amounts**........ Alt + S

    If you do not want amounts rounded to nearest dollar:

    Select **Show Cents in Amounts** .... Alt + S

12. Click **Accounts** .... Alt + A
    in **Customize** box.

13. Select each account to include in report from **Accounts Used** box.

    OR

    Click [🎿 **Mark All**] .... Alt + M

    OR

    Choose one of the following category buttons to select all accounts in that category:

    - [🏛 **Bank**] .... Alt + B

    - [📦 **Cash**] .... Alt + H

Investment Income Report (continued)

- Credit Card .... `Alt` + `D`

- Investment .... `Alt` + `I`

- Asset .... `Alt` + `S`

- Liability .... `Alt` + `Y`

NOTE: *If one or more accounts are selected which you wish to deselect, click them in the* ***Accounts Used*** *box.*

14. Click **Transactions** .... `Alt` + `N`
    in **Customize** box.

15. Click **Unrealized Gains**, if desired.

16. Click **Show Rows** .... `Alt` + `R`
    in **Customize** box.

17. Click **Transfers** box .... `Alt` + `T`

18. Select desired transfers option .... `↓` `↑`
    from list.

19. Click **Select to Include** .... `Alt` + `C`

20. Choose one of the following **Include** options:

    - Actions .... `Alt` + `I`

    - Categories .... `Alt` + `E`

    - Securities .... `Alt` + `S`

    - Security Types .... `Alt` + `T`

continued...

Investment Income Report (continued)

- Investment Goals .... `Alt` + `V`

21. Click each option to include from **Select to Include** box.

If there are more than seven options to choose from, the Select to Include box becomes a scroll box.

OR

Click `Mark All` .... `Alt` + `M`

> *NOTE:* *If one or more options are selected which you wish to deselect, click them in the* ***Select to Include*** *scroll box.*

22. Click **Matching** .... `Alt` + `G` in **Customize** box.

Matching allows you to filter transactions appearing in reports based on a specific characteristic of a payee, category, class, memo or security.

23. Click **Security Contains** box .... `Alt` + `Y`

24. Type security name .... *name* in dialog box.

OR

Select security from box .... `↓` `↑`

25. Click **Memo** .... `Alt` + `M` and type memo, if desired.

26. Click `✔ OK` .... `↵`

INVESTMENT PERFORMANCE REPORT

Create Investment Income Report

1. Click **Reports**

2. Click **Investment** .... `Alt` + `I`

3. Click **Investment Performance** .... `Tab`, `↓` `↑`

4. Click **Customize** .... `Alt` + `C`

5. Select desired report dates from **Report Dates** list.
   OR

   a. Click **from** box .... `Alt` + `F`
      and enter date.

   b. Click **to** box................................... `Alt` + `O`
      and enter date.

   NOTE: *At the **from** and **to** boxes, you can also*
   access the drop-down calendar from which
   you can select starting and ending dates.

6. Click **Title** box .... `Alt` + `I`

7. Type report title... *title*

8. Click **Subtotal By** box .... `Alt` + `U`

9. Select subtotal option from list

   If you want amounts rounded to nearest dollar:

   Deselect **Show Cents in Amounts** .... `Alt` + `S`

continued...

146

Create Investment Income Report (continued)

If you do not want amounts rounded to nearest dollar:

Deselect **Show Cents in Amounts**........ `Alt` + `S`

If you want report to show cash flow detail:

Select **Cash Flow Detail** .... `Alt` + `W`

If you do not want report to show cash flow detail:

Deselect **Cash Flow Detail** .... `Alt` + `W`

10. Click **Accounts** .... `Alt` + `A`
    in **Customize** box.

11. Click each account to include in report from **Accounts Used** box.

    Click **Mark All** .... `Alt` + `M`

    OR

    Choose one of the following category buttons to select all accounts in that category:

    - **Bank** .... `Alt` + `B`

    - **Cash** .... `Alt` + `H`

    - **Credit Card** .... `Alt` + `D`

continue

147

Create Investment Income Report (continued)

- **Investment** .... `Alt` + `I`

- **Asset** .... `Alt` + `S`

- **Liability** .... `Alt` + `Y`

> NOTE: If one or more accounts are selected which you wish to deselect, click them in the **Accounts Used** box.

12. Click **Transactions** .... `Alt` + `N`

13. Click **Tax-related Transactions Only**... `Alt` + `X` if desired.

14. Click **Select to Include** .... `Alt` + `C`

15. Choose one of the following **Include** options:

- **Securities** .... `Alt` + `S`

- **Security Types** .... `Alt` + `T`

- **Investment Goals** .... `Alt` + `V`

16. Click each option to include in report from **Select to Include** box.

*If there are more than seven options to choose from, the **Select to Include** box becomes a scroll box.*

OR

Click **Mark All** .... `Alt` + `M`

> NOTE: If one or more options are selected which you wish to deselect, click them in the **Select to Include** scroll box.

continued...

148

Create Investment Income Report (continued)

17. Click **Matching**...................................... `Alt` + `G`
    in **Customize** box.

Matching allows you to filter transactions appearing in reports based on a specific characteristic of a payee, category, class, memo or security.

18. Click **Security Contains** .... `Alt` + `Y`

19. Type security name... *name*
    in dialog box.

    OR

    Select security from box.

20. Click [✔ **OK**] .... `⏎`

INVESTMENT TRANSACTIONS REPORT

Create Investment Transactions Report

1. Click `Reports`

2. Click **Investment** .... `Alt` + `I`

3. Click **Investment Transactions**.

4. Click `Customize` .... `Alt` + `C`

5. Select desired report dates from **Report Dates** list.

   OR

   a. Click **from** box .... `Alt` + `F`
      and enter date.

   b. Click **to** box................................. `Alt` + `O`
      and enter date.

   *NOTE: At the **from** and **to** boxes, you can also
           access the drop-down calendar from which
           you can select starting and ending dates.*

6. Click **Title** box .... `Alt` + `I`

7. Type report title .... *title*

8. Click **Subtotal By** box.......................... `Alt` + `U`

9. Select subtotal option from list.

10. Click **Organization** box....................... `Alt` + `Z`

continued...

Create Investment Transactions Report (continued)

11. Choose one of the following **Organization** options:

    - Income and Expense
    - Cash flow basis

    If you want amounts rounded to nearest dollar:

    Deselect **Show Cents in Amounts**........ `Alt` + `S`

    If you do not want amounts rounded to nearest dollar:

    Select **Show Cents in Amounts** .... `Alt` + `S`

12. Click **Accounts** .... `Alt` + `A`

13. Select each account to include in report from **Accounts Used** box.

If you have more than seven Quicken accounts, the Accounts Used box displays a scroll bar enabling you to access all reports.

    OR

    Click [💰 **Mark All**] .... `Alt` + `M`

    OR

    Choose one of the following category buttons to select all accounts in that category:

    - [🏛 **Bank**] .... `Alt` + `B`

    - [🏠 **Cash**] .... `Alt` + `H`

    - [CREDIT **Credit Card**] .... `Alt` + `D`

continu

Create Investment Transactions Report (continued)

- ![STOCK] **Investment** .... `Alt` + `I`

- ![🏠] **Asset** .... `Alt` + `S`

- ![🚗] **Liability** .... `Alt` + `Y`

NOTE: *If one or more accounts are selected which you wish to deselect, click them in the **Accounts Used** box.*

14. Click **Transactions** .... `Alt` + `N`

15. Choose one or more of the following options, if desired:

    - Include **U**nrealized Gains .... `Alt` + `U`

    - Ta**x**–related Transactions Only .... `Alt` + `X`

16. Click **Show Rows** .... `Alt` + `R`
    in **Customize** box.

17. Click **Transfers** box .... `Alt` + `T`

18. Select desired transfers option from list.

19. Click **Select to Include** .... `Alt` + `C`

20. Choose one of the following **Include** options:

    - Act**i**ons .... `Alt` + `I`

    - Cat**e**gories .... `Alt` + `E`

    - **S**ecurities .... `Alt` + `S`

continued...

Create Investment Transactions Report (continued)

- Security Types .... `Alt` + `T`

- Investment Goals .... `Alt` + `V`

21. Click each option to include from **Select to Include** box.

    OR

    Click `Mark All` .... `Alt` + `M`

    NOTE: *If one or more options are selected which you wish to deselect, click them in the* **Select to Include** *scroll box.*

22. Click **Matching** .... `Alt` + `G`
    in **Customize** box.

Matching allows you to filter transactions appearing in reports based on a specific characteristic of a payee, category, class, memo or security.

23. Click **Security Contains** .... `Alt` + `Y`
    box.

24. Type security name .... *name*
    in dialog box.

    OR

    Select security from box.

25. Click **Memo** .... `Alt` + `M`
    and type memo, if desired.

26. Click **OK** .... ✔ OK

ITEMIZED CATEGORIES REPORT

Create Itemized Categories Report

1. Click [Reports]

2. Click **Home**...[Alt] + [H]

3. Click **Itemized Categories**................[Tab], [↓] [↑]

4. Click [Customize].............................[Alt] + [C]

5. Select desired report dates from **Report Dates** list.

   OR

   a. Click **from** box...........................[Alt] + [F]
      and enter date.

   b. Click **to** box.............................[Alt] + [O]
      and enter date.

   NOTE: At the from and to boxes, you can also access the drop-down calendar from which you can select starting and ending dates.

6. Click **Title** box................................[Alt] + [I]

7. Type report title................................... *title*

8. Click **Subtotal By** box.......................[Alt] + [U]

9. Select desired **Subtotal By** option from list.

10. Click **Sort By** box............................[Alt] + [B]

11. Select desired **Sort By** option from list.

continued...

154

Create Itemized Categories Report (continued)

12. Click **Organization** box .... `Alt` + `Z`

13. Choose one of the following **Organization** options:
    - Income & expense
    - Cash flow basis

14. Select/deselect desired **Show** options:

    - Cents in Amounts .... `Alt` + `S`

    - Totals Only .... `Alt` + `Y`

    - Memo .... `Alt` + `M`

    - Category .... `Alt` + `E`

    - Split Transaction Detail .... `Alt` + `P`

15. Click **Accounts** .... `Alt` + `A`
    in **Customize** box.

16. Select each account to include in report from
    Accounts Used box.

    OR

    Click ▟ **Mark All** .... `Alt` + `M`

    OR

    Choose one of the following **Accounts Used**
    buttons to select all accounts in that category:

    - 🏛 **Bank** .... `Alt` + `B`

continu

Create Itemized Categories Report (continued)

- ![Cash icon] **Cash** .... `Alt` + `H`

- ![Credit Card icon] **Credit Card** .... `Alt` + `D`

- ![Investment icon] **Investment** .... `Alt` + `I`

- ![Asset icon] **Asset** .... `Alt` + `S`

- ![Liability icon] **Liability** .... `Alt` + `Y`

> *NOTE:* *If one or more accounts are selected which you wish to deselect, click them in the* ***Accounts Used*** *box.*

17. Click **Transactions** .... `Alt` + `N`
    in **Transaction** box.

18. Click **Amounts** box .... `Alt` + `M`

19. Choose one of the following **Amounts** options:
    - **All**
    - Go to step 21.
    - **less than**
    - **equal to**
    - **greater than**

20. Click blank box to right of **Amounts** box.

21. Enter desired amount .... *amount*
    relative to option you chose in step 18.

    > *NOTE:* *For example, if you want the report to display only transactions of less than fifty dollars, you would choose* ***less than*** *in step 18, and enter* 50 *in step 20*

continued...

Create Itemized Categories Report (continued)

22. Choose one or more of the following options, if desired:

   - Include Underalized Gains .... `Alt` + `U`
   - Tax–related Transactions Only .... `Alt` + `X`

23. Click **Transaction Types** box .... `Alt` + `T`

24. Select desired transaction type to appear in report from list.

25. Select one or more of the following **Status** options, if desired:

   - Blank .... `Alt` + `B`
   - Newly Cleared .... `Alt` + `W`
   - Reconciled .... `Alt` + `E`

The default values for the above options are preselected.

   NOTE: To deselect any of the above options, click them.

26. Click **Show Rows** .... `Alt` + `R`
   in **Customize** box.

27. Click **Transfers** box .... `Alt` + `T`

28. Select desired **Transfers** option from list.

29. Click **Subcategories** box .... `Alt` + `S`

30. Select desired **Subcategories** option from list.

31. Click **Categories/Classes** .... `Alt` + `C`
   in **Customize** box.

continu

Create Itemized Categories Report (continued)

32. Choose one of the following options:

- Categories .... **Alt** + **E**

- Classes .... **Alt** + **S**

Categories is the default above.

33. Click each category or class to include from **Select to Include** box.

> *NOTE:* *For categories, the **Select to Include** box is a scroll box. If you have created more than seven classes, the **Select to Include** box also becomes a scroll box.*

OR

Click [**Mark All**] .... **Alt** + **M**

> *NOTE:* *If one or more categories or classes are selected which you wish to deselect, click them in the **Select to Include** scroll box.*

34. Click **Matching** .... **Alt** + **G** in **Customize** box.

Matching allows you to filter transactions appearing in reports based on a specific characteristic of a payee, category, class, memo or security.

35. Click **Payee Contains** box .... **Alt** + **P**

continued...

158

Create Itemized Categories Report (continued)

36. Type payee name .... *name*
    in dialog box.

    OR

    Select payee from box.

37. Click **Category Contains** box .... `Alt` + `E`

38. Type category name .... *name*
    in dialog box.

    OR

    Select category from box.

39. Click **Class Contains** box. .... `Alt` + `S`

40. Type class name .... *name*
    in dialog box.

    OR

    Select class from box.

41. Click **Memo** .... `Alt` + `M`
    and type memo, if desired.

42. Click **OK** .... ✔ OK

JOB/PROJECT BUSINESS REPORT

Create Job/Project Business Report

1. Click **Reports**

2. Click **Business**............................ `Alt` + `B`

3. Click **Job/Project**..................... `Tab`, `↓` `↑`

4. Click **Customize**........................ `Alt` + `C`

5. Select desired report dates from **Report Dates** list.

   OR

   a. Click **from** box........................ `Alt` + `F`
      and enter date.

   b. Click **to** box............................ `Alt` + `O`
      and enter date.

   *NOTE: At the **from** and **to** boxes, you can also
   access the drop-down calendar from
   which you can select starting and ending
   dates.*

6. Click **Title** box........................ `Alt` + `I`

7. Type report title.............................. *title*

8. Click **Row** box.......................... `Alt` + `W`

9. Select desired row heading option from list.

10. Click **Column** box..................... `Alt` + `U`

continued...

Create Job/Project Business Report (continued)

11. Select desired column heading option from list.

12. Click **Organization** box .... `Alt` + `Z`

13. Choose one of the following **Organization** options:

    - Income & expense
    - Cash flow basis

    If you want amounts rounded to nearest dollar:

    Deselect **Show Cents in Amounts** .... `Alt` + `S`

    If you do not want amounts rounded to nearest dollar:

    Select **Show Cents in Amounts** .... `Alt` + `S`

    If you want amounts displayed as percentage of whole:

    Select **Amount as %** .... `Alt` + `%`

14. Click **Accounts** .... `Alt` + `A`
    in **Customize** box.

15. Select each account to include in report from **Accounts Used** box.

    OR

    Click 🖌 **Mark All** .... `Alt` + `M`

    OR

    Choose one of the following **Accounts Used** buttons to select all accounts in that category:

continue

Create Job/Project Business Report (continued)

- 🏛 **Bank** .... Alt + B
- 🏦 **Cash** .... Alt + H
- 💳 **Credit Card** .... Alt + D
- 📈 **Investment** .... Alt + I
- 🏠 **Asset** .... Alt + S
- 🚗 **Liability** .... Alt + Y

NOTE: *If one or more accounts are selected which you wish to deselect, click them in the* ***Accounts Used*** *box.*

16. Click **Transactions** .... Alt + N
    in **Customize** box.

17. Click **Amounts** box .... Alt + M

18. Choose one of the following **Amounts** options:

    - **All**

      Go to step 21.

    - **less than**

    - **equal to**

    - **greater than**

19. Click blank box to right of **Amounts** box.

20. Enter desired amount .... *amount*
    relative to option you
    chose in step 18.

continued...

Create Job/Project Business Report (continued)

NOTE: *For example, if you want the report to display only transactions of less than fifty dollars, you would choose **less than** in step 18, and type 50 in step 20.*

21. Choose one or more of the following options, if desired:

    • Include Unrealized Gains................. `Alt` + `U`

    • Tax–related Transactions Only........ `Alt` + `X`

22. Click **Transaction Types**...................... `Alt` + `T`
    box.

23. Select desired transaction type to appear in report from list.

24. Select one or more of the following status options, if desired:

    • Blank.. `Alt` + `B`

    • Newly Cleared .... `Alt` + `W`

    • Reconciled .... `Alt` + `E`

The default values for the above options are preselected.

   NOTE: *To deselect any of the above options, click them.*

25. Click **Show Rows** .... `Alt` + `R`
    in **Customize** box.

26. Click **Transfers** box............................... `Alt` + `T`

continu

Create Job/Project Business Report (continued)

27. Select desired **Transfers** option from list.

28. Click **Subcategories** box .... Alt + S

29. Select desired **Subcategories** option from list.

30. Click **Categories/Classes** .... Alt + C

31. Choose one of the following options:

- Categories .... Alt + E

- Classes .... Alt + S

Categories is the default above.

32. Click each category or class to include from **Select to Include** box.

For categories, the Select to Include box is a scroll box. If you have created more than seven classes, the Select to Include box also becomes a scroll box.

OR

Click .... Alt + M

NOTE: *If one or more categories or classes are selected which you wish to deselect, click them in the Select to Include scroll box.*

33. Click **Matching** .... Alt + G
    in **Customize** box.

Matching allows you to filter transactions appearing in reports based on a specific characteristic of a payee, category, class, memo or security.

continued...

164

Create Job/Project Business Report (continued)

34. Click **Payee Contains** .... **Alt** + **P**
    box.

35. Type payee name .... *name*
    in dialog box.

    OR

    Select payee from box.

36. Click **Category Contains** .... **Alt** + **E**
    box.

37. Type category name .... *name*
    in dialog box.

    OR

    Select category from box.

38. Click **Class Contains** box .... **Alt** + **S**

39. Type class name .... *name*
    in dialog box.

    OR

    Select class from box.

40. Press **Tab** .... **Tab**

41. Click **Memo** .... **Alt** + **M**
    and type memo, if desired.

42. Click [✔ OK] .... ↵

continu

MARK TRANSACTIONS

Clears transactions your bank has processed.

Mark Single Transaction as Cleared

1. Highlight bank account containing transaction you want to clear in **Account List**.

2. Click **Open** .... **Alt** + **P**

3. Click **Activities** .... **Alt** + **V**, **C**

4. Enter appropriate information in **Reconcile Bank Statement** window.

5. Click [✔ **OK**] . ... **↵**

The Reconcile Bank Account window appears, displaying lists of payments and deposits not yet cleared.

To mark transaction as cleared:

a. Click transaction.

b. Click [**Mark All**] .... **Alt** + **M**

OR
Click transaction.

6. Click [✔ **Done**] .... **Alt** + **D**

> *NOTE:* *If the account does not balance, Quicken will notify you to either continue the reconciliation process or allow Quicken to adjust the balance for you.*

Mark Range of Transactions as Cleared

1. Highlight account containing transaction you want to clear.

2. Click  Open .... Alt + O

3. Click **Activities**................................... Alt + A

4. Click **Reconcile**.. C

5. Enter information in **Reconcile Bank Statement** dialog box.

6. Click ✔ OK .... ↵

The Reconcile Bank Account window appears, showing lists of payments and deposits not yet cleared.

7. Click first transaction to mark as cleared.

8. Hold mouse button down and drag to last transaction to mark as cleared.

9. Release mouse button.

All transactions are marked as cleared, from the one you clicked to the one you released the mouse over.

> NOTE: If the account does not balance, Quicken will notify you to either continue the reconciliation process or allow Quicken to adjust the balance for you.

MEMORIZED REPORTS

Memorizes report instructions for frequently used reports. Useful for customized reports, especially those using filters.

(See CUSTOMIZE REPORT, page 89, for instructions on how to customize reports.)

Memorize Report

1. Create customized report.

2. Click `H✓ Memorize` .... `Alt` + `M`

3. Type title... *title* of memorized report.

4. Choose one of the following date options:

   - Named Range................................. `Alt` + `A`

   - Custom.. `Alt` + `C`

   - None; Use Report Default............... `Alt` + `N`

5. Click `✔ OK` .... `↵`

   > NOTE: When Quicken memorizes a report, it does not memorize the date range, dollar amounts or printer settings.

Recall Memorized Report

1. Click **Reports** menu............................. `Alt` + `R`

2. Click **Memorized** .... `M`

3. Double–click memorized report to use.

continued...

Recall Memorized Report (continued)

To change report preferences:

Click `⌐▲ Options` .... `Alt` + `P`
in **Report** window.

4. Click `✔ OK` .... `↵`

Delete Memorized Report

1. Click **Reports** menu .... `Alt` + `R`

2. Click **Memorized** .... `M`

3. Highlight memorized report .... `↓` `↑`
   to delete.

4. Click `🚫 Delete` .... `Alt` + `D`

5. Click `✔ OK` .... `↵`

Rename Memorized Report

1. Click **Reports** menu .... `Alt` + `R`

2. Click **Memorized** .... `M`

3. Highlight memorized report .... `↓` `↑`
   to rename.

4. Click `🖾 Edit` .... `Alt` + `I`

5. Type new name................................. *name*

6. Click `✔ OK` .... `↵`

MEMORIZE TRANSACTIONS

Stores check or register transactions entered in your accounts.

*NOTE: All transactions are automatically memorized if you have **Automatic Memorization of New Transactions** turned on. This is the default setting.*

Delete Memorized Transaction

1. Click **L**ists menu .... `Alt` + `L`

2. Click **Memorized Transaction** .... `T`

3. Highlight memorized transaction .... `↓` `↑`
   to delete.

4. Click `⊘ Delete` .... `Alt` + `D`

5. Click `✔ OK` .... `↵`

Edit Memorized Transaction

1. Click **L**ist menu .... `Alt` + `L`

2. Click **Memorized Transaction** .... `T`

3. Select memorized transaction to edit.

4. Click `✎ Edit` .... `Alt` + `I`

5. Make necessary changes to transaction.

6. Click `✔ OK` .... `↵`

Memorize Transaction Manually

1. Open register or **Write Checks** window of account containing transaction you want to memorize.

2. Enter information to memorize in register or **Write Checks** window.

3. Press **Ctrl+M** .... `Ctrl` + `M`

   OR

   a. Click [🖎 Edit] .... `Alt` + `I`

   b. Click **Memorize Transaction** .... `M`

4. Click [🖎 Edit] .... `Alt` + `I`

Print Memorized Transaction List

1. Click **Lists** menu .... `Alt` + `L`

2. Click **Memorized Transaction** .... `T`

3. Click **File** .... `Alt` + `F`

4. Click **Print List** .... `P`

5. Select desired print options.

6. Click [🖶 Print] .... `Alt` + `P`

Recall Memorized Transaction

1. Open register or **Write Checks** window of account containing transaction you want to memorize.

2. Click **Lists** menu .... `Alt` + `L`

3. Click **Memorized Transaction** .... `T`

4. Highlight memorized transaction............... `↓` `↑`
   you want to recall.

5. Click `☞ Use` .... `Alt` + `U`

6. Add any necessary information to recalled
   transaction.

7. Click `Record` .... `Alt` + `C`

Turn Off Automatic Memorization of Transactions

—WITH AN ACCOUNT OPEN—

1. Click `Options` .... `Alt` + `P`
   on button bar.

2. Click **QuickFill**................................. `Alt` + `K`

3. Click **Automatic Memorization** .... `Alt` + `A`
   of New Transactions.

   *NOTE: The above step deselects the option box.
   If there is no check in the box, automatic
   memorization is already off.*

4. Click `✔ OK` .... `↵`

MONTHLY BUDGET REPORT

1. Click Reports

2. Click **Home** .... B

3. Click **Monthly Budget** .... B

4. Click Reports .... Alt + C

5. Select desired report dates from **Report Dates** list.

   OR

   a. Click **from** box .... Alt + F
      and enter date.

   b. Click **to** box .... Alt + O
      and enter date.

   NOTE: *At the **from** and **to** boxes, you can also*
   access the drop–down calendar from
   which you can select starting and ending
   dates.

6. Click **Title** box...................................... Alt + I

7. Type report title ....*title*

8. Click **Column** box.

9. Select desired column heading option from list.

10. Click **Organization** box .... Alt + Z

continu

Monthly Budget Report (continued)

11. Choose one of the following **Organization** options:

    - Income & expense
    - Cash flow basis

    If you want amounts rounded to nearest dollar:

    Deselect **Show Cents in Amounts** .... Alt + S

    If you do not want amounts rounded to nearest dollar:

    Select **Show Cents in Amounts** .... Alt + S

12. Click **Accounts** .... Alt + A
    in **Customize** box.

13. Select each account to include from **Accounts Used** box.

    OR

    Click  .... Alt + M

    OR

    Click one of the following **Accounts Used** buttons to select all accounts in that category:

    -  .... Alt + B

    - Cash .... Alt + H

    - Credit Card .... Alt + D

    - Investment .... Alt + I

continued...

Monthly Budget Report (continued)

- 🏠 **A̲s̲set** .... Alt + S

- 🚗 **Liabilit̲y̲** .... Alt + Y

    NOTE: *If one or more accounts are selected which*
    you wish to deselect, click them in the
    Accounts Used *box.*

14. Click **Transaction̲s̲** .... Alt + N
    in **Customize** box.

15. Click **A̲m̲ounts** box .... Alt + M

16. Choose one of the following **A̲m̲ounts** options:

    - **All**

        Go to step 19.

    - **less than**

    - **equal to**

    - **greater than**

17. Click blank box to right of **A̲m̲ounts** box.

18. Enter desired amount ....*amount*
    relative to option you
    chose in step 16.

    NOTE: *For example, if you wanted the report to*
    display only transactions of less than fifty
    dollars, you would choose ***less than*** *in*
    step 16, and type 50 *in step 18.*

19. Choose one or more of the following options, if
    desired:

continue

Monthly Budget Report (continued)

- Include <u>U</u>nrealized Gains .... `Alt` + `U`

- Ta<u>x</u>–related Transactions Only .... `Alt` + `X`

20. Click **Transaction <u>T</u>ypes** box .... `Alt` + `T`

21. Select desired transaction type .... `↓` `↑`
    list.

22. Select one or more of the following status options,
    if desired:

- <u>B</u>lank .... `Alt` + `B`

- Ne<u>w</u>ly Cleared .... `Alt` + `W`

- R<u>e</u>conciled .... `Alt` + `E`

Default values for the above options are preselected.

    NOTE: To deselect any of the above options, click
             them.

23. Click **Show <u>R</u>ows** .... `Alt` + `R`
    in **Customize** box.

24. Click **<u>T</u>ransfers** box .... `Alt` + `T`

25. Select desired **<u>T</u>ransfers** option .... `↓` `↑`

26. Click **<u>S</u>ubcategories** box .... `Alt` + `S`

27. Select desired **<u>S</u>ubcategories** option .... `↓` `↑`

28. Click **Cat<u>e</u>gories** box .... `Alt` + `E`

continued...

Monthly Budget Report (continued)

29. Select desired **Categories** option............... [↓] [↑]

30. Click **Categories/Classes** .... [Alt] + [C]
    in **Customize** box.

31. Choose one of the following options:

    • Categories....................................... [Alt] + [E]

    • Classes .... [Alt] + [S]

Categories is the default above.

32. Click each category or class to include from **Select to Include** box.

*For categories, the **Select to Include** box is a scroll box. If you have created more than seven classes, the **Select to Include** box also becomes a scroll box.*

OR

Click [🖌 **Mark All**] .... [Alt] + [M]

> NOTE: If one or more categories or classes are selected which you wish to deselect, click them in the **Select to Include** scroll box.

33. Click **Matching**................................ [Alt] + [G]
    in **Customize** box.

Matching allows you to filter transactions appearing in reports based on a specific characteristic of a payee, category, class, memo or security.

34. Click **Payee Contains** box................... [Alt] + [P]

continu

Monthly Budget Report (continued)

35. Type payee name.. *name*
    in dialog box.

    OR

    Select payee from box.

36. Cllck **Cat_egory Contains** box............... Alt + E

37. Type category name .... *name*
    in dialog box.

    OR

    Select category from box.

38. Click **Cla_ss Contains** .... Alt + S
    box.

39. Type class name... *name*
    in dialog box.

    OR

    Select category from box.

40. Click **_Memo** .... Alt + M
    and type memo, if desired.

41. Click [✔ OK] .... ↵

NET WORTH REPORT

Create Net Worth Report

1. Click **Reports**

2. Click **Home** .... `Alt` + `B`

3. Click **Net Worth** .... `Tab`, `↓` `↑`

4. Click **Customize** .... `Alt` + `C`

5. Select desired report dates from **Report Dates** list.

   OR

   a. Click **from** box .... `Alt` + `F`
      and enter date.

   b. Click **to** box.................................. `Alt` + `O`
      and enter date.

   NOTE: *At the **from** and **to** boxes, you can also*
            access the drop–down calendar from
            which you can select starting and ending
            dates.

6. Click **Title** box................................ `Alt` + `I`

7. Type report title ....*title*

8. Click **Interval** box .... `Alt` + `V`

9. Select desired interval option from **Interval** list.

10. Click **Organization** box .... `Alt` + `Z`

continu

Create Net Worth Report (continued)

11. Choose one of the following **Organization** options:
    - Net worth
    - Balance sheet

    If you want amounts rounded to nearest dollar:

    Deselect **Show Cents in Amounts** .... Alt + S

    If you do not want amounts rounded to nearest dollar:

    Select **Show Cents in Amounts** .... Alt + S

12. Click **Accounts** .... Alt + A
    in **Customize** box.

13. Select each account to include from **Accounts Used** box.

    OR

    Click  .... Alt + M

    OR

    Click one of the following **Accounts Used** buttons to select all accounts in that category:

    -  .... Alt + B

    - Cash .... Alt + H

    - Credit Card .... Alt + D

    - Investment .... Alt + I

continued...

Create Net Worth Report (continued)

- | 🏠 **A_sset** | .... Alt + S
- | 🚗 **Liability** | .... Alt + Y

> *NOTE:* *If one or more accounts are selected which*
> *you wish to deselect, click them in the*
> ***Accounts Used*** *box.*

14. Click **Transactions** .... Alt + N
    in **Customize** box.

15. Click **A_mounts** box .... Alt + M

16. Choose one of the following **A_mounts** options:

    - **All**

      Go to step 19.

    - **less than**

    - **equal to**

    - **greater than**

17. Click blank box to right of **A_mounts** box.

18. Enter desired amount ....*amount*
    relative to option you
    chose in step 16.

    > *NOTE:* *For example, if you want the report to*
    > *display only transactions of less than fifty*
    > *dollars, you would choose **less than** in*
    > *step 16, and type 50 in step 18.*

continu

Create Net Worth Report (continued)

19. Choose one or more of the following options, if desired:

   - Include Unrealized Gains .... `Alt` + `U`

   - Tax–related Transactions Only .... `Alt` + `X`

20. Click **Transaction Types** box .... `Alt` + `T`

21. Select desired transaction type to appear from list.

22. Select one or more of the following status options, if desired:

   - Blank .... `Alt` + `B`

   - Newly Cleared .... `Alt` + `W`

   - Reconciled .... `Alt` + `E`

The default values for the above options are preselected.

> NOTE: To deselect any of the above options, click them.

23. Click **Show Rows** .... `Alt` + `R`
   in **Customize** box.

24. Click **Subcategories** box .... `Alt` + `S`

25. Select desired **Subcategories** option from list.

26. Click **Categories/Classes** .... `Alt` + `C`
   in **Customize** box.

continued...

Create Net Worth Report (continued)

27. Choose one of the following options:

- Categories.. Alt + E

- Classes .... Alt + S

Categories is the default above.

28. Click each category or class from **Select to Include** box.

For categories, the Select to Include box is a scroll box. If you have created more than seven classes, the Select to Include box also becomes a scroll box.

OR

Click [Mark All] .... Alt + M

NOTE: *If one or more categories or classes are selected which you wish to deselect, click them in the Select to Include scroll box.*

29. Click **Matching**................................ Alt + G

Matching allows you to filter transactions appearing in reports based on a specific characteristic of a payee, category, class, memo or security.

30. Click **Payee Contains**.......................... Alt + P box.

31. Type payee name .... *name* in dialog box.

OR

Select payee from box.

32. Click **Category Contains** box .... Alt + E

continu

Create Net Worth Report (continued)

33. Type category name .... *name*
    in dialog box.

    OR

    Select category from box.

34. Click **Cla_s_s Contains** box .... Alt + S

35. Type class name... *name*
    in dialog box.

    OR

    Select category from box.

36. Click **Memo** .... Alt + M
    and type memo, if desired.

37. Click [✔ **OK**] .... ↵

184

ORDER CHECKS

Intuit (the makers of Quicken) carries a line of supplies that can be used in conjunction with Quicken, including checks, double-window envelopes, endorsement stamps, and many other products. To order these supplies, print a supply order form.

1. Click **Activities**................................... **Alt** + **V**

2. Click **Order Checks**.

3. Click

The Print Supplies Order Form window appears.

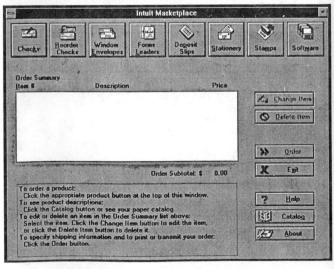

4. Select desired options.

continu

Order Checks (continued)

Checks	Alt + K
Reorder Checks	Alt + R
Window Envelopes	Alt + E
Forms Leaders	Alt + L
Deposit Slips	Alt + P
Stationery	Alt + S
Stamps	Alt + M
Software	Alt + W

5. Click `>> Order` .... Alt + O
   when finished.

6. Click `X Exit` .... Alt + X
   to return to program.

PASSWORD

Set File Password

1. Open file you want to password protect.

2. Click **F**ile .... Alt + F

3. Click **P**asswords .... A

4. Click **F**ile .... F

5. Type password .... *password*
   (maximum of 16 characters).

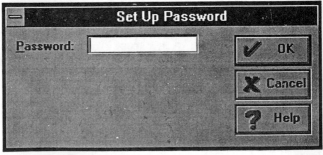

6. Click ✔ OK .... ↵

7. Retype password .... *password*
   to confirm.

8. Click ✔ OK .... ↵

Change/Remove File Password

1. Open file whose password you want to change.

2. Click **F**ile .... Alt + F

3. Click **P**asswords .... A

Change/Remove File Password (continued)

4. Click **File** .... **F**

5. Type **Old Password** .... *password*

6. Press **Tab** .... **Tab**

7. Type **New Password** .... *password*
   (maximum of 16 characters).

   OR

   Leave blank to remove password.

8. Click **✔ OK** .... **↵**

9. Retype new password .... *password*
   to confirm.

If you removed password, you'll return to program.

10. Click **✔ OK** .... **↵**

Set Transaction Password

1. Click **File** .... **Alt** + **F**

2. Click **Passwords** .... **A**

3. Click **Transaction** .... **T**

4. Type password .... *password*
   (maximum of 16 characters).

5. Press **Tab** .... **Tab**

continued...

Set Transaction Password (continued)

6. Enter date ....*date*
   through which password is required.

7. Click [✔ OK] ....[↵]

8. Retype new password..........................*password*
   to confirm.

9. Click [✔ OK] ....[↵]

Change or Remove Transaction Password

1. Click **F**ile..[Alt] + [F]

2. Click **P**asswords ....[A]

3. Click **T**ransaction..[T]

4. Type old password..........................*password*

5. Press **Tab** ....[Tab]

   If you want to change password:

   a. Type new password ....*password*
      (maximum of 16 characters).

   b. Enter date ....*date*
      through which new password is required.

   c. Click [✔ OK] ....[↵]

   d. Retype new password..........................*password*
      to confirm.

   e. Click [✔ OK] ....[↵]

   If you want to remove password:

   Click [✔ OK] ....[↵]

   NOTE: Leave **new password** field blank.

PAYROLL REPORT

Create Payroll Report

1. Click

2. Click **Business**.. B

3. Click **Payroll**.................................... Tab , ↓ ↑

4. Click  .... Alt + C

5. Select desired report dates from **Report Dates** list.

   OR

   a. Click **from** box.............................. Alt + F
      and enter date.

   b. Click **to** box................................... Alt + O
      and enter date.

   NOTE: *At the **from** and **to** boxes, you can also*
            access the drop–down calendar from
            which you can select starting and ending
            dates.

6. Click **Title** box................................... Alt + I

7. Type report title.. *title*

8. Click **Row** box.................................... Alt + W

9. Select desired row heading option .... ↓ ↑

continued...

Create Payroll Report (continued)

10. Click **Column** box............................ `Alt` + `U`

11. Select desired column heading option....... `↓` `↑`

12. Click **Organization** box .... `Alt` + `Z`

13. Choose one of the following **Organization** options:
    - Income & expense
    - Cash flow basis

    If you want amounts rounded to nearest dollar:

    Deselect **Show Cents in Amounts**........ `Alt` + `S`

    If you do not want amounts rounded to nearest dollar:

    Select **Show Cents in Amounts** .... `Alt` + `S`

    If you want amounts displayed as percentage of whole:

    Select **Amount as %** .... `Alt` + `%`

14. Click **Accounts** .... `Alt` + `A`
    in **Customize** box.

15. Select each account to include from **Accounts Used** box.

    OR

    Click [**Mark All**] .... `Alt` + `M`

    OR

    Click one of the following **Accounts Used** buttons to select all accounts in that category:

continue

Create Payroll Report (continued)

- | 🏛 **B**ank | .... | Alt + B |

- | 🏦 Ca**s**h | .... | Alt + H |

- | 💳 Cre**d**it Card | .... | Alt + D |

- | 📈 **I**nvestment | .... | Alt + I |

- | 🏠 A**s**set | .... | Alt + S |

- | 🚗 Liabilit**y** | .... | Alt + Y |

NOTE: *If one or more accounts are selected which you wish to deselect, click them in the* ***Accounts Used*** *box.*

16. Click **Transactio̲ns** .... Alt + N
    in **Customize** box.

17. Click **A̲mounts** box .... Alt + M

18. Choose one of the following **A̲mounts** options:

    - **All**

      Go to step 21.

    - **less than**

    - **equal to**

    - **greater than**

19. Click blank box to right of **A̲mounts** box.

20. Enter desired amount .... *amount*
    relative to option you
    chose in step 18.

continued...

Create Payroll Report (continued)

> *NOTE:* *For example, if you want the report to display only transactions of less than fifty dollars, you would choose **less than** in step 18, and type 50 in step 20.*

21. Choose one or more of the following options, if desired:

- Include Unrealized Gains.................. `Alt` + `U`

- Tax–related Transactions Only .... `Alt` + `X`

22. Click **Transaction Types** box .... `Alt` + `T`

23. Select desired transaction type from list.

24. Select one or more of the following **Status** options, if desired:

- Blank... `Alt` + `B`

- Newly Cleared .... `Alt` + `W`

- Reconciled .... `Alt` + `E`

The default values for the above options are preselected.

> *NOTE:* *To deselect any of the above options, click them.*

25. Click **Show Rows** .... `Alt` + `R`
    in **Customize** box.

26. Click **Transfers** box............................. `Alt` + `T`

27. Select desired **Transfers** option from list.

28. Click **Subcategories** box..................... `Alt` + `S`

continu

Create Payroll Report (continued)

29. Select desired **Subcategories** option list.

30. Click **Categories/Classes** .... `Alt` + `C`
    in **Customize** box.

31. Choose one of the following options:

    - Categories .... `Alt` + `E`

    - Classes .... `Alt` + `S`

Categories is the default above.

32. Click each category or class to include in **Select to Include** box.

For categories, the Select to Include box is a scroll box. If you have created more than seven classes, the Select to Include box also becomes a scroll box.

    OR

    Click [**Mark All**] .... `Alt` + `M`

    NOTE: If one or more categories or classes are selected which you wish to deselect, click them in the Select to Include scroll box.

33. Click **Matching** .... `Alt` + `G`

Matching allows you to filter transactions appearing in reports based on a specific characteristic of a payee, category, class, memo or security.

34. Click **Payee Contains** .... `Alt` + `P`
    box.

continued...

Create Payroll Report (continued)

35. Type payee name .... *name*
    in dialog box.

    OR

    Select payee from box.

36. Click **Cat<u>e</u>gory Contains** box .... Alt + E

37. Type category name .... *name*
    in dialog box.

    OR

    Select category from box.

38. Click **Cla<u>s</u>s Contains** .... Alt + S
    box.

39. Type class name .... *name*
    in dialog box.

    OR

    Select class from box.

40. Click **<u>M</u>emo** .... Alt + M
    and type memo,
    if desired.

41. Click [✔ OK] .... ⏎

PORTFOLIO VALUE REPORT

Create Portfolio Value Report

1. Click **Reports**

2. Click **Investment** .... `Alt` + `I`

3. Click **Portfolio Value** .... `Tab`, `↓` `↑`

4. Click **Customize** .... `Alt` + `C`

5. Select desired report dates from **Report Dates** list.

   OR

   a. Click **from** box.............................. `Alt` + `F`
      and enter date.

   b. Click **to** box................................. `Alt` + `O`
      and enter date.

   NOTE: At the **from** and **to** boxes, you can also
   access the drop-down calendar from
   which you can select starting and ending
   dates.

6. Click **Title** box .... `Alt` + `I`

7. Type report title................................... *title*

8. Click **Subtotal By** box .... `Alt` + `U`

9. Select subtotal option from list.

   If you want amounts rounded to nearest dollar:

   Deselect **Show Cents in Amounts** .... `Alt` + `S`

continued...

Create Portfolio Value Report (continued)

If you do not want amounts rounded to nearest dollar:

Select **Show Cents in Amounts** .... `Alt` + `S`

10. Click **Accounts** .... `Alt` + `A`
    in **Customize** box.

11. Select each account to include from **Accounts Used** box.

    OR

    Click `Mark All` .... `Alt` + `M`

    OR

    Click one of the following category buttons to select all accounts in that category:

    - `Bank` .... `Alt` + `B`

    - `Cash` .... `Alt` + `H`

    - `Credit Card` .... `Alt` + `D`

    - `Investment` .... `Alt` + `I`

    - `Asset` .... `Alt` + `S`

    - `Liability` .... `Alt` + `Y`

    NOTE: If one or more accounts are selected which you wish to deselect, click them in the **Accounts Used** *box.*

12. Click **Transactions** .... `Alt` + `N`
    in **Customize** box.

continu

Create Portfolio Value Report (continued)

13. Click **Tax–related Transactions Only**... `Alt` + `X`
    if desired.

14. Click **Select to Include** .... `Alt` + `C`

15. Choose one of the following **Select to Include**
    options:

    • <u>S</u>ecurities .... `Alt` + `S`

    • Security <u>T</u>ypes................................. `Alt` + `T`

    • In<u>v</u>estment Goals .... `Alt` + `V`

16. Click each **Select to Include** option to include from
    Select to Include box.

    OR

    Click | **M̲ark All** | .... `Alt` + `M`

    *NOTE: If one or more options are selected which
    you wish to deselect, click them in the
    Select to Include scroll box.*

17. Click **Matching** .... `Alt` + `G`

*Matching allows you to filter transactions appearing in reports
based on a specific characteristic of a payee, category, class,
memo or security.*

18. Click **Security Contains**........................ `Alt` + `Y`
    box.

continued...

Create Portfolio Value Report (continued)

19. Type security name.................................... *name*
    in dialog box.

    OR

    Select security from box.

20. Click [✔ **OK**] .... [↵]

POSTDATE CHECKS

Set Reminder of Postdated Checks

1. Click [**Options**]

2. Click **R**eminders .... [Alt] + [E]

3. Click **T**urn on Billminder .... [Alt] + [T]

    *NOTE: The above step selects the **Turn on
    Billminder** box. If there is already a check
    in the box, go directly to step 4.*

4. Press **Tab** .... [Tab]

5. Enter number................................... *number*
   of days in advance you want
   to be reminded of postdated checks.

6. Click [✔ **OK**] .... [↵]

7. Click [➡ **Close**] .... [↵]

PRINT REPORTS

Prints reports on paper or to other files on disk, allowing you to export this information to word processing programs or spreadsheets or preview the report on screen.

1. Create the report you want to print.

2. Click [🖶 Print] .... `Ctrl` + `P`

3. Choose one of the following **Print to** options:

   - Printer .... `Alt` + `R`

   - ASCII Disk File .... `Alt` + `D`

   - Tab–delimited Disk File .... `Alt` + `B`

   - 123 [.PRN] Disk File .... `Alt` + `1`

   - Screen .... `Alt` + `S`

   If you would like negative amounts printed in red:

   Click **Print in color** .... `Alt` + `C`

   NOTE: For the above option, you must have a color printer.

   If you want draft mode printing:

   Click **Print in draft mode** .... `Alt` + `M`

   If you want to print range of pages instead of entire document:

   a. Click **Pages** .... `Alt` + `G`

   b. Click **From** field .... `Alt` + `F`

continued...

Print Reports (continued)

c. Enter starting page number .... *number*

d. Click **T**o field .... Alt + T

e. Enter ending page number.................. *number*

4. Click 🖨 Pri**n**t .... Alt + P

If you selected to print to an ASCII Disk file, a Tab–delimited Disk File or a 123 [.PRN] Disk File in step 3:

a. Type filename .... *filename* including path.

b. Click ✔ OK .... ↵

PRINT CHECKS

Find Out How Many Checks to Print

1. Open account for which you ant to print checks.

   OR

   a. Highlight account for which you want to print checks.

   b. Click **O**p**e**n .... Alt + P

2. Click **F**ile.. Alt + F

3. Click Print **C**hecks C

At the top of the dialog box, Quicken displays the number of checks to print and for what amount.

Set Printer Settings for Checks

1. Click **File** .... **Alt** + **F**

2. Click **Printer Setup** .... **S**

3. Click **Check Printer Setup** .... **C**

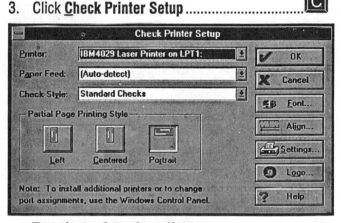

To select printer from list:

a. Click down arrow .... **↓**

b. Highlight desired printer.

NOTE: *If the printer you want to use is not listed,*
*use the Windows **control panel** to install*
the printer driver for your printer. (See
your Microsoft Windows User's Guide for
instructions on installing a printer.)

4. Press **Tab** .... **Tab**
to move to **Paper Feed** box.

5. Press **Tab** .... **Tab**
to leave auto–detect as your paper feed option.

6. Click **Check Style** .... **Alt** + **Y**

continued...

Set Printer Settings for Checks (continued)

7. Select desired check style.......................... `↓` `↑`

8. Choose one of the following **Partial Page Printing Styles**:

   • Left .... `Alt` + `L`

   • Centered .... `Alt` + `C`

   • Portrait.. `Alt` + `R`

   NOTE: Not all of the above options may be available to you, depending on your printer.

9. Click `🖶 Font...` .... `Alt` + `F`

   —FROM CHECK PRINTING FONT WINDOW—

10. Select desired font type, style or size for the printing on your checks.

11. Click `✔ OK` .... `↵`

12. Click `🖶 Settings...` .... `Alt` + `S`
    in dialog box.

    —IN SETUP WINDOW—

13. Set correct paper size, source, resolution, number of copies, printer memory, paper orientation and cartridge choice for check style you are using.

    NOTE: Not all options may be available to you, depending on your printer.

14. Click `✔ OK` twice..................... `↵` , `↵`

Print Sample Checks on Continuous–Feed Printers

Lets you see how your checks are aligned before printing.

1. Insert checks into printer.

2. Double–click account for which you want to print checks.

3. Click **File** .... `Alt` + `F`

4. Click **Print Checks** .... `C`

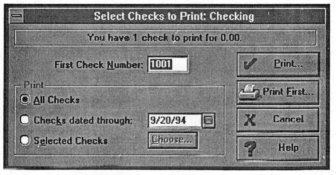

5. Click `Print` .... `Alt` + `P`

6. Select correct check style...... `Alt` + `Y`, `↓` `↑` in **Check Style** list.

7. Click **Print First** .... `Alt` + `F`

   *NOTE: If you receive a message that your check printer is not set up for the form size Quicken requires, click **OK** to print your checks using the default printer font.*

continued...

Print Sample Checks on Continuous–Feed Printers (continued)

If sample check printed correctly:

Click [✔ **OK**].. [↵]

in **Check Printer Setup** window.

If sample check printed incorrectly:

a. Click **A**lign .... [Alt] + [A]

b. Click and drag check fields to position where they appear on your printed sample check.

Quicken realigns the printing of the check to correct the misalignment you show it here.

c. Click **T**est .... [Alt] + [T]

OR

a. Enter correct horizontal .... *measurement* measurement in .01" increments in **H**oriz box.

b. Press **Tab** .... [Tab]

c. Enter correct vertical................... *measurement* measurement in .01" increments in **V**ert box.

d. Click **T**est .... [Alt] + [T]

NOTE: *The positioning should be almost perfect. If a half–line adjustment is needed, use the printer knob to move the check up half a line. Make a note of the correct position for future use.*

8. Click [✔ **OK**] .... [↵]

9. Click [🖨 Pri**n**t] .... [Alt] + [P]

Print Checks on Continuous–Feed Printer

1. Insert checks into printer.

2. Double–click account for which you want to print checks.

3. Click **File** .... `Alt` + `F`

4. Click **Print Checks** .... `C`

5. Enter first check number .... *number*

6. Choose one of the following print options:

    *   **All Checks** .... `Alt` + `A`

    *   **Checks dated through** .... `Alt` + `K`
        to print range of checks.

        a. Press **Tab** .... `Tab`

        b. Enter date .... *date*
            for last check to print.

    *   **Selected Checks** .... `Alt` + `E`
        to print selected checks.

        a. Click **Choose** .... `Alt` + `C`

        b. Click to select .... `↑` `↓`, `Space`
            desired checks.

    *NOTE: A check mark [✔] appears in column to
    the left of selected checks.*

    OR

continued...

Print Checks on Continuous–Feed Printer (continued)

Click [🖊️ **M**ark All] .... [Alt] + [M]
to select all checks.

To check print settings:

a. Click **Print First**.................... [Alt] + [F]

b. Select **CheckStyle**...................... [↓][↑]

c. Click [✔ OK] .... [↵]

d. Click [🖨️ Print] .... [Alt] + [P]

Did Check(s) print OK? window appears.

If checks printed correctly:

Click [✔ OK] .... [↵]

If checks did not print correctly:

a. Enter number.. *number*
of first check printed incorrectly.

b. Click [✔ OK] .... [↵]

Quicken makes incorrectly printed checks available again for printing.

> *NOTE:* You may now adjust the printer or the
> alignment and print the checks again.

Print Sample Checks on Page–Oriented (Laser) Printers

Lets you see how your checks are aligned before printing.

1. Insert checks into printer.

2. Double–click account for which you want to print checks.

3. Click **File** .... `Alt` + `F`

4. Click **Print Checks** .... `C`

5. Click [🖨 Print] .... `Alt` + `P`

6. Make sure correct check style appears in **Check Style** list.

7. Choose one of the following to show Quicken how many checks are on the first page:

   • Three .... `Alt` + `R`

   • Two .... `Alt` + `W`

   • One .... `Alt` + `O`

8. Click [✔ OK] .... `↵`

   NOTE: *If you receive a message that your check printer is not set up for the form size Quicken requires, click **OK** to print your checks using the default printer font.*

   Did checks print correctly? *message appears.*

continued...

Print Sample Checks on Page–Oriented (Laser) Printers (continued)

Click [✔ **OK**] .... [⏎]
if checks printed correctly

If sample check printed correctly:

Click [✔ **OK**] .... [⏎]
in **Check Printer Setup** window.

If sample check printed incorrectly:

a. Click **Align** .... [Alt] + [A]

b. Click and drag check fields to position where they appear on your printed sample check.

Quicken realigns the printing of the check to correct the misalignment you show it here.

c. Click **Test** .... [Alt] + [T]

OR

a. Enter correct horizontal .... *measurement* measurement in .01" increments in **Horiz** box.

b. Press **Tab** .... [Tab]

c. Enter correct vertical.................. *measurement* measurement in .01" increments in **Vert** box.

d. Click **Test** .... [Alt] + [T]

continu

Print Sample Checks on Page–Oriented (Laser) Printers (continued)

NOTE: *The positioning should now be almost perfect. If it is off by a noticeable amount, repeat alignment steps until a sample check prints correctly.*

9. Click **✔ OK** .... **↵**

10. Click **🖨 Print** .... **Alt** + **P**

Test sample check again. Repeat above steps if necessary.

If check printed correctly:

a. Click **Print** .... **Alt** + **P**

NOTE: *Make sure correct style appears in the* **Check Style** *box.*

b. Click **✔ OK** .... **↵**
to print checks.

If check did not print correctly:

a. Enter # of first check .... *number*
that did not print correctly.

b. Click **✔ OK** .... **↵**

c. Click **✖ Cancel** .... **Esc**

d. Click **File** .... **Alt** + **I**

continued...

Print Sample Checks on Page–Oriented (Laser) Printers (continued)

   e. Click **Printer Setup**..............................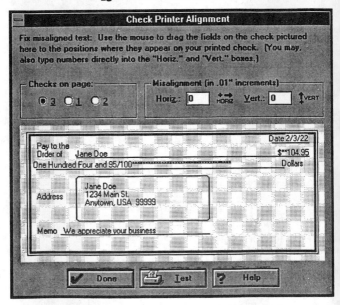

   f. Click **Align**.......................................

Print Checks on Page–Oriented (Laser) Printer

1. Insert one full page of checks into printer.

2. Double–click account for which you want to print checks.

3. Click **File**..

4. Click **Print Checks** ....

continu

Print Checks on Page–Oriented (Laser) Printer
(continued)

5. Enter number ....*number*
   for first check to print
   in **First Check Number** box.

6. Choose one of the following **checks to print**
   options:

   - **All Checks** .... `Alt` + `A`

   - **Checks dated through** .... `Alt` + `K`
     to print range of checks.

     a. Press **Tab** .... `Tab`

     b. Enter date .... *date*
        for last check to print.

   - **Selected Checks** .... `Alt` + `E`
     to print selected checks.

     a. Click **Choose** .... `Alt` + `C`
        OR
        Double–click check to select it for printing.
        OR
        i. Highlight check.

        ii. Press **Spacebar** .... `Space`

     b. Repeat a–b for each check to print.

   *NOTE: All selected checks for printing should be
            marked **print** on the right before preceding
            to step 7.*

     c. Click [✔ OK] .... `↵`

continued...

Print Checks on Page–Oriented (Laser) Printer (continued)

- <u>F</u>irst Check .... `Alt` + `F`

7. Click `🖨 Pri<u>n</u>t` .... `Alt` + `P`

8. Make sure correct style of check is showing in **Check Style** list.

9. Choose one of the following to show Quicken how many checks are on first page:

- <u>T</u>hree .... `Alt` + `T`

- T<u>w</u>o .... `Alt` + `W`

- <u>O</u>ne .... `Alt` + `O`

10. Click `🖨 Pri<u>n</u>t` .... `Alt` + `P`

Did Check(s) print OK? window appears.

If checks printed correctly:

Click `✔ OK` .... `↵`

If checks did not print correctly:

a. Enter number .... *number* of first check printed incorrectly.

b. Click `✔ OK` .... `↵`

Quicken makes incorrectly printed checks available again for printing.

> NOTE: You may now adjust the printer or the alignment, and print the checks again.

PROFIT AND LOSS STATEMENT REPORT

Create Profit and Loss Statement Report

1. Create the report you want to print.

2. Click **Business** .... `Alt` + `B`

3. Click **P & L Statement** .... `Tab`, `↓` `↑`

4. Click `Customize` .... `Alt` + `C`

5. Select desired report dates from **Report Dates** list.

   OR

   a. Click **from** box .... `Alt` + `F`
      and enter date.

   b. Click **to** box .... `Alt` + `O`
      and enter date.

   NOTE: *At the **from** and **to** boxes, you can also*
            access the drop–down calendar from
            which you can select starting and ending
            dates.

6. Click **Title** box .... `Alt` + `I`

7. Type report title .... *title*

8. Click **Row** box .... `Alt` + `W`

9. Select desired row heading option from list.

10. Click **Column** box .... `Alt` + `U`

continued...

Create Profit and Loss Statement Report (continued)

11. Select desired column heading option from list.

12. Click **Organization** box .... Alt + Z

13. Choose one of the following **Organization** options:

    - Income & expense

    - Cash flow basis

    If you want amounts rounded to nearest dollar:

    Deselect **Show Cents in Amounts** .... Alt + S

    If you do not want amounts rounded to nearest dollar:

    Select **Show Cents in Amounts** .... Alt + S

    If you want amounts displayed as percentage of whole:

    Select **Amount as %** .... Alt + %

14. Click **Accounts** .... Alt + A
    in **Customize** box.

15. Select each account to include from **Accounts Used** box.

    OR

    Click [Mark All] .... Alt + M

    OR

    Choose one of the following **Accounts Used** buttons to select all accounts in that category:

continue

Create Profit and Loss Statement Report (continued)

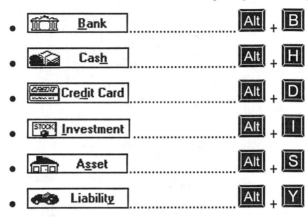

- 🏛 **B**ank .... Alt + B
- 🪙 **Cas**h .... Alt + H
- 💳 **Cre**dit Card .... Alt + D
- 📈 **I**nvestment .... Alt + I
- 🏠 **A**sset .... Alt + S
- 🚗 **Lia**bility .... Alt + Y

*NOTE: If one or more accounts are selected which you wish to deselect, click them in the **Accounts Used** box.*

16. Click **Transactions** .... Alt + N
    in **Customize** box.

17. Click **A**mounts box .... Alt + M

18. Choose one of the following **A**mounts options:

    - **All**

      Go to step 21.

    - **less than**

    - **equal to**

    - **greater than**

19. Click blank box to right of **A**mounts box.

20. Enter desired amount .... *amount*
    relative to option you
    chose in step 18.

continued...

Create Profit and Loss Statement Report (continued)

> *NOTE:* *For example, if you want the report to display only transactions of less than fifty dollars, you would choose **less than** in step 18, and type 50 in step 20.*

21. Choose one or more of the following options, if desired:

   - Include <u>U</u>nrealized Gains................. `Alt` + `U`

   - Ta<u>x</u>–related Transactions Only........ `Alt` + `X`

22. Click **Transaction Types** box .... `Alt` + `T`

23. Select desired transaction type from list.

24. Select one or more of the following status options, if desired:

   - <u>B</u>lank... `Alt` + `B`

   - Ne<u>w</u>ly Cleared .... `Alt` + `W`

   - R<u>e</u>conciled .... `Alt` + `E`

The default values for the above options are preselected.

> *NOTE:* *To deselect any of the above options, click them.*

25. Click **Show Rows** .... `Alt` + `R`
   in **Customize** box.

26. Click **Transfers** box............................. `Alt` + `T`

27. Select desired **Transfers** option from list.

continue•

Create Profit and Loss Statement Report (continued)

28. Click **Subcategories** box .... `Alt` + `S`

29. Select desired **Subcategories** option from list.

30. Click **Categories/Classes** .... `Alt` + `C`
    in **Customize** box.

31. Choose one of the following options:

    • Categories .... `Alt` + `E`

    • Classes .... `Alt` + `S`

Categories is the default above.

32. Click each category or class to include from **Select
    to Include** box.

*For categories, the Select to Include box is a scroll box. If
you have created more than seven classes, the Select to
Include box also becomes a scroll box.*

> **OR**
>
> Click `Mark All` .... `Alt` + `M`
>
> *NOTE: If one or more categories or classes are
> selected which you wish to deselect, click
> them in the Select to Include scroll box.*

33. Click **Matching** .... `Alt` + `G`

*Matching allows you to filter transactions appearing in reports
based on a specific characteristic of a payee, category, class,
memo or security.*

34. Click **Payee Contains** box .... `Alt` + `P`

continued...

218

35. Type payee name .... *name*
    in dialog box.

    OR

    Select payee from box.

36. Click **Category Contains** box .... Alt + E

37. Type category name .... *name*
    in dialog box.

    OR

    Select category from box.

38. Click **Class Contains** .... Alt + S
    box.

39. Type class name .... *name*
    in dialog box.

    OR

    Select class from box.

40. Press **Tab** .... Tab

41. Type memo .... *memo*
    in **Memo Contains** dialog box.

42. Click [✔ OK] .... ↵

QCARDS

Qcards are instructions for certain features usually appearing above or to the side of the current window.

Turn Qcards On/Off

1. Click **Help** .... Alt + H

2. Click **Show Qcards** .... Alt + S

A check mark means the feature is on.

QUICKFILL

*Memorizes a transaction the first time you enter it. After that, QuickFill automatically fills in the transaction information the next time you begin to enter it. If QuickFill fills in the incorrect information, however, you are still able to enter the correct information over it. Any Quicken register or **Write Checks** window must be open*

1. Click ▲ O**p**tions .... Alt + P

2. Click **Quic**k**Fill** .... Alt + K

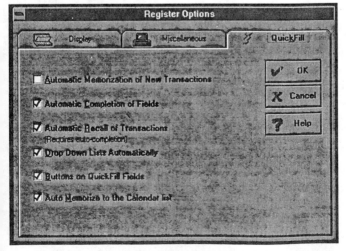

continued...

Quickfill (continued)

3. Choose desired settings:

- <u>A</u>utomatic Memorization .... `Alt` + `A`
  of New Transactions

- Automatic <u>C</u>ompletion of Fields ...... `Alt` + `C`

- Automatic <u>R</u>ecall of Transactions ... `Alt` + `R`

- <u>Dr</u>op Down Lists Automatically .... `Alt` + `D`

- <u>B</u>uttons on QuickFill Fields .... `Alt` + `B`

- Auto <u>M</u>emorize .... `Alt` + `M`

4. Click [✔ OK] .... `↵`

QUICKZOOM

Allows you to view details of an amount represented in a report or graph. When you move the cursor arrow over an amount, if the cursor becomes a magnifying glass, you may use QuickZoom to bring up the register detailing the separate transactions representing that amount.

1. Create desired report or graph.

2. Place cursor on desired amount.

OUTFLOWS	
Ads	123.00
Bus. Utilities	56.00
Outflows - Other	431.67
TO Brokerage	10,188.00
TO Investment	50,000.00
TOTAL OUTFLOWS	60,799.34

NOTE: If the cursor does not become a magnifying glass, you cannot bring up further details on the desired amount.

3. Double–click amount.

RECONCILE ACCOUNTS

Reconcile Bank Account

1. Click  Accts

The Account List appears.

2. Double–click account you want to reconcile.

3. Click **Acti<u>v</u>ities** .... Alt + V

4. Click **Re<u>c</u>oncile** C

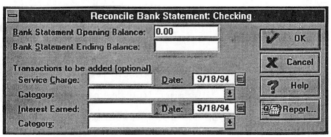

5. Compare bank statement opening balance (shown in window) with opening balance (shown on your bank statement).

   If amounts differ:

   a. Enter opening balance .... *amount* as shown on your statement in **<u>B</u>ank Statement Opening Balance** dialog box.

   b. Choose optional additional transactions:

      • Service <u>C</u>harge & <u>D</u>ate

      • Cate<u>g</u>ory

continued...

Reconcile Bank Account (continued)

- <u>I</u>nterest Earned & D<u>a</u>te
- Categor<u>y</u>

c. Click [✔ **OK**] .... [↵]

The Reconcile Bank Account window appears, listing uncleared transactions separated into payments and deposits.

To list transactions by date:

Select <u>S</u>ort by Date box .... [Alt] + [S]

Quicken's default setting sorts transactions by check number.

If amount on Difference line (lower right–hand corner of **Reconcile Bank Account** window) **is zero (0.00):**

Bank statement and Quicken are reconciled.

If amount on Difference line (lower right–hand corner of **Reconcile Bank Account** window) **is not zero (0.00):**

Click each transaction in reconcile list also appearing on your bank statement (to mark transaction as cleared).

OR

a. Highlight first transaction in reconcile list also appearing on your bank statement.

b. Press **Spacebar** .... [Space]
   to mark transaction as cleared.

   OR

continu

Reconcile Bank Account (continued)

Click **Mark All** .... Alt + M
to mark transaction as cleared.

c. Repeat steps a and b for each transaction on
reconcile list also appearing on your bank
statement.

NOTE: *To deselect a transaction, click it or press*
Spacebar *again.*

6. Click **Done** .... Alt + D

NOTE: *If there is still a difference between your*
bank statement balance and the Quicken
balance, consult your Quicken User's
Guide.

Print Reconciliation Report

1. Reconcile bank account *(see **Reconcile Bank***
***Account**, page 221).*

—*FROM CONGRATULATORY MESSAGE SCREEN*—

2. Click **Yes** .... Alt + Y

3. Type report title .... *title*

NOTE: *The above step is optional.*

4. Press **Tab** .... Tab

5. Type reconcile date .... *date*

6. Choose one of the following options for
transactions to include:

continued...

Print Reconciliation Report (continued)

- Al<u>l</u> Transactions .... `Alt` + `A`

- <u>S</u>ummary and Uncleared .... `Alt` + `S`

7. Click [Pri<u>n</u>t] .... `Alt` + `P`

8. Choose print options.

9. Click [Pri<u>n</u>t] .... `Alt` + `P`

Reconcile Credit Card Account

1. Click [Accts]

The Account List appears.

2. Double–click credit card account you want to reconcile.

3. Click Acti<u>v</u>ities..................................... `Alt` + `V`

4. Click Pay <u>C</u>redit Card Bill.............................. `C`

5. Enter <u>C</u>harges, Cash Advances ....*amount*

6. Click <u>P</u>ayments, Credits .... `Alt` + `P`
   and enter amount.

7. Enter <u>N</u>ew Balance...................................*amount*

8. Enter <u>F</u>inance Charges..............................*amount*

9. Click <u>D</u>ate .... `Alt` + `D`
   and enter date.

continu

Reconcile Credit Card Account (continued)

10. Click **Ca̲tegory** .... *category*
    and enter category.

11. Click ....

    If amount in Difference line (lower right–hand corner of **Pay Credit Card Bill** window) **is zero (0.00):**

    Credit card statement and Quicken are reconciled.

    If amount in Difference line (lower right–hand corner of **Pay Credit Card Bill** window) **is not zero (0.00):**

    Click each transaction in reconcile list also appearing on your credit card statement (to mark transaction as cleared).

    OR

    a. Highlight first transaction in reconcile list also appearing on your credit card statement

    b. Press **Spacebar** .... Space
       to mark transaction as cleared.

       OR

       Click  .... Alt + M
       to mark transaction as cleared.

    c. Repeat steps 11a and 11b for each transaction on reconcile list that appears on your credit card statement.

continued...

226

Reconcile Credit Card Account (continued)

> *NOTE:* *To deselect a transaction, click it or press* ***Spacebar*** *a second time.*

12. Click **D**one ....

> *NOTE:* *If there is still a difference between your credit card statement balance and the Quicken balance, Quicken displays a window asking whether you want to record the difference as an adjustment to Quicken's opening balance, a payment transaction or a charge. (See Quicken User's Guide for instructions on how to adjust the balance.)*

REGISTER

Records transactions in your accounts.

Create New Transaction

1. Click

The Account List appears.

2. Double–click account whose register you need to access.

3. Enter date ....*date* in **date** field.

4. Press **Tab** .... Tab

   If you use handwritten checks:

   Enter check number...................................*number*

   If you do not use handwritten checks:

continu

Create New Transaction (continued)

Leave **NUM** field blank.

5. Press **Tab** .... `Tab`

6. Type identifying name or word .... *name* or *word*
   in **Payee** field.

7. Press **Tab** .... `Tab`

8. Enter payment amount .... *amount*
   in **payment** field.

   OR
   Enter deposit amount .... *amount*
   in **deposit** field.

9. Press **Tab** .... `Tab`

10. Type category .... *category*

11. Press **Tab** .... `Tab`

12. Type **Memo** .... *memo*
    if desired.

13. Press **Tab** .... `Tab`

14. Click `Record` .... `Alt` + `C`

continued...

Delete Transaction

1. Click

The Account List appears.

2. Double–click account whose register you need to access.

3. Highlight transaction to delete.

4. Press 🚫 D̲elete .... Ctrl + D

5. Click Y̲es .... Alt + Y

Print Register

1. Click

The Account List appears.

2. Double–click account whose register you want to print.

   OR
   a. Highlight account whose register you want to print.

   b. Click Op̲en .... Alt + P

3. Press **Ctrl+P** (P̲rint) ....Ctrl + P

   OR
   a. Click F̲ile .... Alt + F

continu

Print Register (continued)

    b. Click **Print Register** .... `P`

4. Enter **from** date .... *date*
    for transactions.

5. Press **Tab** .... `Tab`

6. Enter **to** date .... *date*
    for transactions.

7. Press **Tab** .... `Tab`

8. Type report title .... *title*

    NOTE: *The above step is optional.*

9. Press **Tab** .... `Tab`

10. Choose from the following format options:

    • Print <u>O</u>ne Transaction Per Line .... `Alt` + `O`

    • Print Transaction <u>S</u>plits .... `Alt` + `S`

    • Sort <u>B</u>y Number .... `Alt` + `B`

    NOTE: *If there is already a check in the box, do*
               *not click it unless you **do not** want that*
               format.

11. Click Pri<u>n</u>t .... `Alt` + `P`

12. Choose to print to one of the following options:

    • P<u>r</u>inter .... `Alt` + `R`

    • ASCII <u>D</u>isk File .... `Alt` + `D`

    • Ta<u>b</u>–delimited Disk File .... `Alt` + `B`

    • <u>1</u>23[.PRN] Disk File .... `Alt` + `1`

    • <u>S</u>creen .... `Alt` + `S`

continued...

Print Register (continued)

13. Click [🖨 Pri_n_t] .... **Alt** + **P**
If you chose to print to disk:

  a. Type filename .... *filename*
  including path.

  b. Click [✔ OK] .... ⏎

RESTORE FILE

1. Click **F**ile .... **Alt** + **F**

2. Click **R**estore .... **R**

3. Insert backup diskette into floppy drive.

4. Type drive letter ....*letter*

5. Click [✔ OK] .... ⏎

—*FROM FILES LIST*—

6. Highlight name of file to restore.

7. Click [✔ OK] .... ⏎

SECURITIES

Add New Security

1. Click **Lists** .... 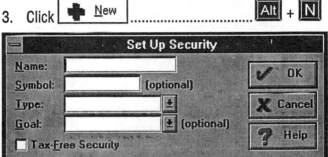 Alt + L

2. Click **Security** .... S

3. Click [✚ New] .... Alt + N

Set Up Security	
Name: [　　　　　　]	✔ OK
Symbol: [　　　] [optional]	
Type: [　　　] ▼	✘ Cancel
Goal: [　　　] ▼ [optional]	
☐ Tax-Free Security	? Help
Est. Annual Income($): [0.00] [per share]	

4. Type new security name .... *name*

5. Press **Tab** .... Tab

6. Type new security symbol .... *symbol*

   NOTE: The above step is optional.

7. Press **Tab** .... Tab

8. Type security type .... *type*

   OR

   a. Click down arrow .... ↓
      to select from list.

continued...

Add New Security (continued)

    b. Highlight security type. ....*type*

9. Press **Tab** .... `Tab`

10. Enter goal ....*goal*

    OR

    a. Click down arrow
       to select from list.

    b. Highlight goal.

    NOTE: The above step is optional.

11. Press **Tab** .... `Tab`

12. Enter estimated annual income................. number

13. Click [✔ OK] .... `↵`

Edit Security

1. Click **Lists** .... `Alt` + `L`

2. Click **Security** .... `S`

3. Highlight security to edit.

4. Click **Edit** .... `Alt` + `I`

5. Make necessary changes in appropriate fields
   (name, type, symbol and/or goal).

6. Click [✔ OK] .... `↵`

Delete Security

1. Click **L**ists... Alt + L

2. Click **S**ecurity... S

3. Highlight security to delete.

4. Click **Del**.. Alt + D

5. Click [✔ OK]... ↵

SELECT ACCOUNTS

If Account List window is not open:

Press **Ctrl+A**.. Ctrl + A

OR

a. Click **L**ists................................. Alt + L

b. Click **A**ccount List.............................. A

Double–click account you want to access.

OR

1. Highlight account you want to access.

2. Click **U**se... Alt + U

SNAPSHOTS

Display overview of any area of your finances that you want to view.

Create Snapshot

1. Click  .... Alt + R, S

The First Page Snapshot appears.

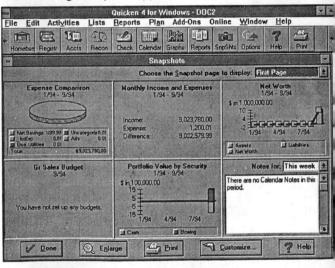

2. Click Snapshot you wish to customize.

   OR

   a. Click Customize .... Alt + C

continu

Create Snapshot (continued)

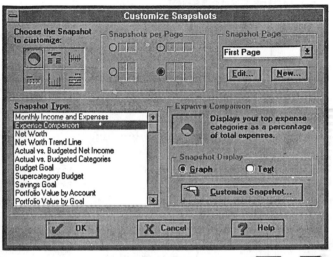

b. Click **Choose the Snapshot** .... `Alt` + `Z`
   to Customize.

3. Click **Snapshot Type** .... `Alt` + `T`
   and select desired type.

4. Click 🔧 **Customize** .... `Alt` + `C`

5. Make desired changes.

6. Click ✔ **OK** .... `↵`
   to return to **Customize Snapshots** dialog box.

7. Click ✔ **OK** .... `↵`
   to return to **Snapshots** window.

   To enlarge selected snapshot:

   a. Click 🔍 **Enlarge** .... `Alt` + `N`

   b. Make desired changes.

8. Click 🚪 **Close** when finished.

236

Edit/Delete Snapshot

1. Click **SnpShts** .... `Alt` + `R`, `S`

2. Click **Customize** .... `Alt` + `C`

3. Click **Snapshot Page** .... `Alt` + `P`
   and select desired page.

4. Click **Edit** .... `Alt` + `E`

5. Highlight desired page .... `↓` `↑`

6. Click **Edit** .... `Alt` + `E`
   to change name.

   OR

   Click **Delete** .... `Alt` + `D`
   to delete.

7. Click **OK** .... `↵`
   when finished.

SPLIT TRANSACTIONS
Assigns more than one category to a transaction.

Split Transaction

1. Click [Accts]

The Account List appears.

2. Double–click account containing transaction to split.

3. Enter information into appropriate fields.

   NOTE: You may want to wait to enter category, payment or deposit information until after the split.

4. Click [Splits] .... Alt + S

The Splits window appears. Any information already entered in the category, payment or deposit fields of the transaction is copied to the first line of the split.

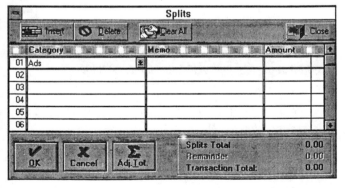

continued...

238

Split Transaction (continued)

If you have not entered category information:

Type first category or class name.................*name*

OR

  a. Click down arrow..⬇
     to select from list.

  b. Highlight category or class.

5. Press **Tab** ....Tab

6. Type memo...*memo*
   in **Memo** field.

   NOTE: The above step is optional.

7. Press **Tab** ....Tab

8. Enter amount...*amount*
   to apply to first category.

   *NOTE: If an amount is already displayed in the
   amount field, you can type over it.*

9. Press **Tab** ....Tab

*The difference between the amount in the transaction and the
amount in the first part of the split appears in the second
amount field.*

10. Repeat steps 4–9 for each category to assign to
    transaction.

    **If you notice a remainder between Splits Total
    and Transaction Total** (lower right–hand corner of
    Splits window):

Split Transaction (continued)

Click 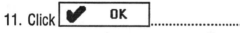 .... Alt + T

OR

Continue. You can also make the adjustment in step 11.

> *NOTE:* *If the remainder is a positive amount, Quicken adjusts the total by creating a new uncategorized split transaction. If you wish, enter a category in the **Category** field.*

11. Click **✔ OK** .... ⏎

> *NOTE:* *Usually the amounts in the split transaction add up to the amount in the register **Amount** field. Sometimes, however, as a result of either deleting an item from the split or adding an item that causes the total to exceed that in the register, the amounts are not equal.*

If amounts in split transaction do not equal amount in register Amount field:

a. Choose one of the following options from **Split Adjustment** window:

- **Adjust Transaction Total** .... Alt + A
  to change transaction total to match split items total.

continued...

Split Transaction (continued)

- **C**reate a Balancing Split Item... `Alt` + `C`
  to create uncategorized split item to balance transaction.

b. Click `✔ OK` .... `←`

If you did not enter amount in register Payment or Deposit fields before opening Splits window:

a. Choose one of the following from **Payment** or **Deposit** window:

- **P**ayment.................................. `Alt` + `P`
- **D**eposit.................................. `Alt` + `D`

b. Click `✔ OK` .... `←`

12. Click `Record` .... `Alt` + `C`

Edit Split Transaction

1. Click `Accts`

The Account List appears.

2. Double–click account to edit.

3. Highlight desired transaction.

4. Click `Splits` .... `Alt` + `S`

5. Make changes in **Split Transaction** window.

6. Click `✔ OK` .... `←`

7. Click `Record` .... `Alt` + `C`

Delete Line in Split Transaction

1. Click

The Account List appears.

2. Double–click account containing split transaction to edit.

3. Highlight desired transaction.

4. Click  .... Alt + S

5. Click any of fields in line you want to delete in **Split Transaction** window.

6. Press 🚫 D̲elete .... Ctrl + D

7. Click ✔ OK .... ↵

8. Click 💾 Record .... Alt + C

Remove Splits from Transaction

1. Click

The Account List appears.

2. Double–click account containing split transaction to edit.

3. Highlight desired transaction.

continued...

242

Remove Splits from Transaction (continued)

4. Click **Splits** .... Alt + S

5. Click **Clear All** .... Alt + C

6. Click **Yes** .... Alt + Y
   in **Delete all split lines?** box.

7. Click **OK** .... ↵

8. Click **Record** .... Alt + C

Use Percentages in Split Transaction

Allows you to enter a split transaction in percentages of the total transaction instead of dollar amounts.

1. Click **Accts**

The Account List appears.

2. Double–click account containing transaction to split.

3. Enter information into appropriate fields.

   *CAUTION: Enter the total transaction amount in the **Payment** or **Deposit** field.*

4. Click **Splits** .... Alt + S

5. Click **Amount** field in first line of **Splits** window.

continu

Use Percentages in Split Transaction (continued)

6. Enter percentage ....*percentage*
   in **Amount** field (e.g. 60%).

   NOTE: Type over dollar amount displayed.

7. Click **Amount** field in next line of **Splits** window.

8. Enter percentage ....*percentage*
   for second part of split.

9. Repeat steps 7 and 8 for any other parts of split
   transaction.

10. Click ✔ **OK** .... Alt + O

11. Click **Edit** .... Alt + E

12. Click **Memorize Transaction** .... M

13. Click **Yes** .... Y
    in **Memorize splits
    as percentages?** window.

14. Click **Yes** .... Alt + Y

15. Click ✔ **OK** .... ↵

Recall Memorized Split Transaction with Percentages

1. Click

The Account List appears.

2. Double–click account containing split transaction.

continued...

244

3. Go to new transaction line.

4. Begin typing payee name in **Payee** field.

Quicken fills in the rest of the name.

5. Press **Tab** .... `Tab`

6. Enter total transaction amount ....*amount* in **Percentage Split** window.

7. Click [✔ **OK**] .... `↵`

Quicken enters the total amount you typed in and splits it into previously entered percentages.

8. Click [**Record**] .... `Alt` + `C`

START QUICKEN

1. Start Windows.

2. Double–click [Quicken]

3. Double–click [Quicken 4 for Windows]

SUBCATEGORIES

Create Subcategory

1. Click **L**ists menu .... `Alt` + `L`

2. Click **C**ategory & Transfer .... `C`

3. Click **N**ew .... `Alt` + `N`

4. Type subcategory name .... *name*
   in **Setup Category** window.

5. Press **Tab** .... `Tab`

6. Type description .... *description*
   NOTE: The above step is optional.

7. Press **Tab** .... `Tab`

8. Select type:
   - **I**ncome
   - **E**xpense

9. Click **S**ubcategory of .... `Alt` + `U`

10. Select parent category from list.

11. Click desired parent category.

   If subcategory is tax–related:

   Click **T**ax–related .... `Alt` + `T`

12. Click [✔ OK] .... `↵`

Change Category to Subcategory

1. Click **L**ists .... `Alt` + `L`

2. Click **C**ategory & Transfer List .... `C`

3. Highlight category you want to change to subcategory.

4. Click [🏠 Edit] .... `Alt` + `I`

5. Click S**u**bcategory of .... `Alt` + `U`

6. Select parent category from list.

7. Click desired parent category.

   If subcategory is tax–related:

   Click **T**ax–related .... `Alt` + `T`

8. Click [✔ OK] .... `↵`

Change Subcategory to Category

1. Click **L**ists .... `Alt` + `L`

2. Click **C**ategory & Transfer List .... `C`

3. Highlight subcategory you want to change to a category.

4. Click [🏠 Edit] .... `Alt` + `I`

   If it is an income category:

   Click **I**ncome .... `Alt` + `I`

continue▸

Change Subcategory to Category (continued)

If it is an expense category:

Click **E**xpense .... `Alt` + `E`

If subcategory is tax–related:

Click **T**ax–related .... `Alt` + `T`

5. Click [✔ **OK**] .... `↵`

SUBCLASSES

Create Subclass

1. Click **L**ists .... `Alt` + `L`

2. Click C**l**ass .... `L`

3. Click **N**ew .... `Alt` + `N`

4. Type subclass name .... *name*
   in **Set Up Class** window.

5. Press **Tab** .... `Tab`

6. Type description .... *description*

   NOTE: The above step is optional.

7. Click [✔ **OK**] .... `↵`

Assign Subclass to Transaction

1. Open register for account containing (or about to contain) transaction to which you want to assign subclass.

2. Enter number (optional), description, amount and memo (optional) in register.

   —IN CATEGORY FIELD—

3. Type category name .... *name*

4. Press **/** (slash) .... **/**

5. Type class name .... *name*

6. Press **:** (colon) .... **:**

7. Type subclass name .... *name*

   EXAMPLE: Utilities/Main Street:Unit 3.

8. Click **Record** .... **Alt** + **C**

9. Click **✔ OK** .... **↵**

Edit Subclass

1. Click **Lists** menu .... **Alt** + **L**

2. Click **Class** .... **L**

3. Highlight subclass to edit.

4. Click **✎ Edit** .... **Alt** + **I**

5. Make necessary changes in **Edit Class** window.

6. Click **✔ OK** .... **↵**

Delete Subclass

1. Click **Lists**.. Alt + L

2. Click **Class** L

3. Highlight subclass to delete.

4. Click | 🚫 Delete | .... Alt + D

5. Click | ✔ OK | .... ↵

SUMMARY REPORT

Create Summary Report

1. Click ☐ Reports

2. Click **Oth̲er** .... Alt + E

3. Click **Summary** .... Tab + ↓ ↑

4. Click 🖱 **Customize** .... Alt + C

5. Select report dates from **Report Dates** list.

   OR

   a. Click **f̲rom** box .... Alt + F
      and enter date.

   b. Click **t̲o** box.................................... Alt + O
      and enter date.

   NOTE: *At the f̲rom and t̲o boxes, you can also*
   access the drop-down calendar from which
   you can select starting and ending dates.

6. Click **Ti̲tle** box...................................... Alt + I

7. Type report title .... *title*

8. Click **Ro̲w** box....................................... Alt + W

9. Select desired **Ro̲w** option from list.

continu

Create Summary Report (continued)

10. Click **Column** box .... ⌨ Alt + U

11. Select desired **Column** option from list.

12. Click **Organization** box .... ⌨ Alt + Z

13. Choose one of the following **Organization** options:

    - Income & Expense

    - Cash flow basis

    If you want amounts rounded to nearest dollar:

    Deselect **Show Cents in Amounts** .... ⌨ Alt + S

    If you do not want amounts rounded to nearest dollar:

    Select **Show Cents in Amounts** .... ⌨ Alt + S

    If you want to display amounts as percentage of whole:

    Select **Amount as %** .... ⌨ Alt + %

14. Click **Accounts** .... ⌨ Alt + A
    in **Customize** box.

15. Select each account to include from **Accounts Used** box.

    OR

    Click [*Mark All*] .... ⌨ Alt + M

    OR

continued...

Create Summary Report (continued)

Choose one of the following **Accounts Used** buttons to select all accounts in that category:

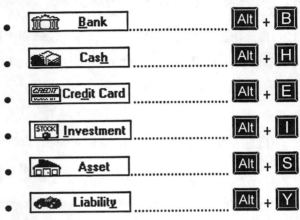

- **Bank** .... Alt + B
- **Cash** .... Alt + H
- **Credit Card** .... Alt + E
- **Investment** .... Alt + I
- **Asset** .... Alt + S
- **Liability** .... Alt + Y

*NOTE: If one or more accounts are selected which you wish to deselect, click them in the **Accounts Used** box.*

16. Click **Transactions**............................... Alt + N
    in **Customize** box.

17. Click **Amounts** box.............................. Alt + M

18. Choose one of the following **Amounts** options:

- **All**

   Go to step 21.

- **less than**

- **equal to**

- **greater than**

Create Summary Report (continued)

19. Click blank box to right of **A̲mounts** box.

20. Enter desired amount .... *amount*
    relative to option you
    chose in step 18.

    *NOTE: For example, if you want the report to
    display only transactions of less than fifty
    dollars, you would choose **less than** in
    step 18, and type 50 in step 20.*

21. Choose one or more of the following options, if
    desired:

    • Include U̲nrealized Gains................ `Alt` + `U`

    • Ta̲x-related Transactions Only .... `Alt` + `X`

22. Click **Transaction T̲ypes** box................ `Alt` + `T`

23. Select desired transaction type to appear in report
    from list.

24. Choose one or more of the following status
    options, if desired:

    • B̲lank.. `Alt` + `B`

    • New̲ly Cleared .... `Alt` + `W`

    • R̲econciled .... `Alt` + `E`

Default values for the above options are preselected.

    *NOTE: To deselect any of the above options, click
    them.*

continued...

Create Summary Report (continued)

25. Click **Show Rows** .... `Alt` + `R`

26. Click **Transfers** box.............................. `Alt` + `T`

27. Select desired **Transfers** option from list.

28. Click **Subcategories** box...................... `Alt` + `S`

29. Select desired subcategories option from list.

30. Click **Categories/Classes** .... `Alt` + `C`
    in **Customize** box.

31. Choose one of the following options:

    • Categories .... `Alt` + `E`

    • Classes.................................... `Alt` + `S`

    Categories is the default above.

32. Click each category or class to include from **Select to Include** box.

    OR

    Click `Mark All` .... `Alt` + `M`

    *NOTE: If one or more categories or classes are selected which you wish to deselect, click them in the **Select to Include** scroll box.*

33. Click **Matching**.................................. `Alt` + `G`
    in **Customize** box.

continu

Create Summary Report (continued)

Matching allows you to filter transactions appearing in reports based on a specific characteristic of a payee, category, class, memo or security.

34. Click **Payee Contains** .... **Alt** + **P**

35. Type payee name... *name*
    in dialog box.

    OR

    Select payee from box.

36. Click **Category Contains**...................... **Alt** + **E**

37. Type category name .... *name*
    in dialog box.

    OR

    Select category from box.

38. Click **Class Contains** box .... **Alt** + **S**

39. Type class name... *name*
    in dialog box.

    OR

    Select class from box.

40. Press **Tab** .... **Tab**

41. Type memo .... *text*
    in **Memo Contains** dialog box.

42. Click [✔ OK] .... **↵**

continued...

TAX PLANNER

Calculates how much tax you will owe at the end of a year.

Helps you determine various tax-related information including tax owed, withholding, estimated taxes and the tax implications of major decisions.

> *CAUTION:* *You must contact Quicken Tax Rate Information line to update changes that occur in 1994/95 tax rate after August 1, 1994. Consult your Quicken documentation for more information.*

1. Click **Pl<u>a</u>n** .... + [A]

2. Click **<u>T</u>ax Planner** .... [T]

The Tax Planner Window appears.

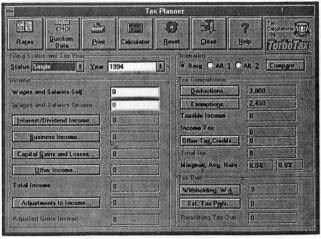

continu

Tax Planner (continued)

Rates	Change rates to current tax year.	**Reset**	Reset values to zero.
Quicken 1040 Data	Import your data into planner.	**Close**	Exit planner.
Print	Print desired form and schedule.	**Help**	Get help with planner.
Calculator	Calculate and copy into fields.		

TAX SCHEDULE REPORT

Create Tax Schedule Report

1. Click **Reports**

2. Click **Home** .... Alt + H

3. Click **Tax Schedule** .... Tab + ↓ ↑

4. Click **Customize** .... Alt + C

5. Select desired report dates from **Report Dates** list.

   OR

continued...

Create Tax Schedule Report (continued)

   a. Click <u>f</u>rom box .... `Alt` + `F`
      and enter date.

   b. Click t<u>o</u> box.................................... `Alt` + `O`
      and enter date.

   NOTE: *At the <u>f</u>rom and t<u>o</u> boxes, you can also access the drop-down calendar from which you can select starting and ending dates.*

6. Click **T<u>i</u>tle** box................................... `Alt` + `I`

7. Type report title .... *title*

8. Click **S<u>u</u>btotal By** box .... `Alt` + `U`

9. Select desired **S<u>u</u>btotal By** option from list.

10. Click **Sort <u>B</u>y** box .... `Alt` + `B`

11. Select desired **Sort <u>B</u>y** option from list.

12. Click **Organi<u>z</u>ation** box .... `Alt` + `Z`

13. Choose one of the following **Organi<u>z</u>ation** options:

   •   Income & expense

   •   Cash flow basis

If you want amounts rounded to nearest dollar:

Deselect **Show Cents in Amount<u>s</u>** .... `Alt` + `S`

continu

Create Tax Schedule Report (continued)

If you do not want amounts rounded to nearest dollar:

Select **Show Cents in Amounts**............ `Alt` + `S`

If you want report to contain only totals:

Select **Totals Only**............................... `Alt` + `Y`

If you want report to contain memo:

Select **Memo** .... `Alt` + `M`

If you do not want report to contain memo:

Deselect **Memo** .... `Alt` + `M`

If you want report to show category:

Select **Category**................................... `Alt` + `E`

If you do not want report to show category:

Deselect **Category** .... `Alt` + `E`

If you want report to show split transaction detail:

Select **Split Transaction Detail**............ `Alt` + `P`

14. Click **Accounts**............................ .... `Alt` + `A`
    in **Customize** box.

continued...

Create Tax Schedule Report (continued)

15. Select each account to include from **Accounts Used** box.

    OR

    Click [**Mark All**] .... `Alt` + `M`

    OR

    Choose one of the following **Accounts Used** buttons to select all accounts in that category:

    - [**Bank**] .... `Alt` + `B`

    - [**Cash**] .... `Alt` + `H`

    - [**Credit Card**] .... `Alt` + `E`

    - [**Investment**] .... `Alt` + `I`

    - [**Asset**] .... `Alt` + `S`

    - [**Liability**] .... `Alt` + `Y`

    *NOTE: If one or more accounts are selected which you wish to deselect, click them in the **Accounts Used** box.*

16. Click **Transactions** .... `Alt` + `N`
    in **Customize** box.

17. Click **Amounts** box .... `Alt` + `M`

continue

Create Tax Schedule Report (continued)

18. Choose one of the following **Amounts** options:

   - **All**

      Go to step 21.

   - **less than**

   - **equal to**

   - **greater than**

19. Click blank box to right of **Amounts** box.

20. Enter desired amount ....*number* relative to option you chose in step 18.

   NOTE: *For example, if you want the report to display only transactions of **less than** fifty dollars, you would choose less than in step 18, and type 50 in step 20.*

21. Choose one or more of the following options, if desired:

   - Include Unrealized Gains................ `Alt` + `U`

   - Tax-related Transactions Only .... `Alt` + `X`

22. Click **Transaction Types** box................ `Alt` + `T`

23. Select desired transaction type to appear from list.

24. Choose one or more of the following status options, if desired:

   - Blank................................... `Alt` + `B`

   - Newly Cleared .... `Alt` + `W`

continued...

Create Tax Schedule Report (continued)

- Reconciled .... Alt + E

Default values for the above options are preselected.

> NOTE: To deselect any of the above options, click
> them.

25. Click **Show Rows** .... Alt + R
    in **Customize** box.

26. Click **Transfers** box............................ Alt + T

27. Select desired transfers option from list.

28. Click **Subcategories** box...................... Alt + S

29. Select desired **Subcategories** option from list.

30. Click **Categories/Classes** .... Alt + C

31. Choose one of the following options:

    - Categories .... Alt + E

    - Classes.. Alt + S

Categories is the default above.

32. Click each category or class to include from **Select
    to Include** box.

*For categories, the Select to Include box is a scroll box. If
you have created more than seven classes, the Select to
Include box also becomes a scroll box.*

> **OR**
>
> Click [Mark All] .... Alt + M

continu

Create Tax Schedule Report (continued)

> *NOTE:* *If one or more categories or classes are selected which you wish to deselect, click them in the **Select to Include** scroll box.*

33. Click **Matching** .... `Alt` + `G`
    in **Customize** box.

Matching allows you to filter transactions appearing in reports based on a specific characteristic of a payee, category, class, memo or security.

34. Click **Payee Contains** box .... `Alt` + `P`

35. Type payee name... *name*
    in dialog box.

    OR

    Select payee from box.

36. Click **Category Contains** box .... `Alt` + `E`

37. Type category name .... *name*
    in dialog box.

    OR

    Select category from box.

38. Click **Class Contains** .... `Alt` + `S`

39. Type class name.. *name*
    in dialog box.

    OR

    Select class from box.

40. Press **Tab** .... `Tab`

continued...

Create Tax Schedule Report (continued)

41. Type memo .... *data*
    in **Memo Contains** dialog box.

42. Click [✔ OK] .... [←]

TAX SUMMARY REPORT

Create Tax Summary Report

1. Click [Reports]

2. Click **Home** .... [Alt] + [H]

3. Click **Tax Summary** .... [Tab] + [↓][↑]

4. Click [✎ Customize] .... [Alt] + [C]

5. Select desired report dates from **Report Dates** list.
   OR

   a. Click **from** box .... [Alt] + [F]
      and enter date.

   b. Click **to** box............................... [Alt] + [O]
      and enter date.

   *NOTE: At the **from** and **to** boxes, you can also*
   access the drop-down calendar from which
   you can select starting and ending dates.

6. Click **Title** box.............................. [Alt] + [I]

7. Type report title .... *title*

8. Click **Subtotal By** box .... [Alt] + [U]

Create Tax Summary Report (continued)

9. Select desired **Subtotal By** option from list.

10. Click **Sort By** box .... `Alt` + `B`

11. Select desired **Sort By** option from list.

12. Click **Organization** box .... `Alt` + `Z`

13. Choose one of the following **Organization** options:

- Income & expense

- Cash flow basis

If you want amounts rounded to nearest dollar:

Deselect **Show Cents in Amounts** .... `Alt` + `S`

If you do not want amounts rounded to nearest dollar:

Select **Show Cents in Amounts** .... `Alt` + `S`

If you want report to contain only totals:

Select **Totals Only** .... `Alt` + `Y`

If you want report to contain memo:

Select **Memo** .... `Alt` + `M`

If you do not want report to contain memo:

Deselect **Memo** .... `Alt` + `M`

If you want report to show category:

Select **Category** .... `Alt` + `E`

continued...

Create Tax Summary Report (continued)

If you do not want report to show category:

Deselect **Cate͟gory** .... Alt + E

If you want report to show split transaction detail:

Select **S͟plit Transaction Detail** .... Alt + P

14. Click **A͟ccounts** .... Alt + A
    in **Customize** box.

15. Select each account to include from **Accounts Used**
    box.

    OR

    Click [💰 **M͟ark All**] .... Alt + M

    OR

    Choose one of the following **Accounts Used**
    buttons to select all accounts in that category:

    - [🏛 **B͟ank**] .... Alt + B

    - [💵 **Cas͟h**] .... Alt + H

    - [💳 **Cre͟dit Card**] .... Alt + E

    - [📈 **I͟nvestment**] .... Alt + I

    - [🏠 **A͟s͟set**] .... Alt + S

    - [🚚 **Liabilit͟y**] .... Alt + Y

    *NOTE: If one or more accounts are selected which
    you wish to deselect, click them in the*

contin▸

Accounts Used box.

Create Tax Summary Report (continued)

16. Click **Transactions** ....<kbd>Alt</kbd> + <kbd>N</kbd>
    in **Customize** box.

17. Click **Amounts** box ....<kbd>Alt</kbd> + <kbd>M</kbd>

18. Choose one of the following **Amounts** options:

    - **All**

      Go to step 21.

    - **less than**

    - **equal to**

    - **greater than**

19. Click blank box to right of **Amounts** box.

20. Enter desired amount ....*number*
    relative to option you chose in step 18.

    *NOTE: For example, if you want the report to
    display only transactions of less than fifty
    dollars, you would choose **less than** in
    step 19, and type 50 in step 20.*

21. Choose one or more of the following options, if
    desired:

    - Include **U**nrealized Gains.................<kbd>Alt</kbd> + <kbd>U</kbd>

    - Ta**x**-related Transactions Only ....<kbd>Alt</kbd> + <kbd>X</kbd>

22. Click **Transaction Types**.....................<kbd>Alt</kbd> + <kbd>T</kbd>

23. Select desired transaction type to appear from list.

continued...

Create Tax Summary Report (continued)

24. Choose one or more of the following status options, if desired:

- Blank .... `Alt` + `B`

- Newly Cleared .... `Alt` + `W`

- Reconciled .... `Alt` + `E`

Default values for the above options are preselected.

> NOTE: *To deselect any of the above options, click them.*

25. Click **Show Rows** .... `Alt` + `R`
    in **Customize** box.

26. Click **Transfers** box................. `Alt` + `T`

27. Select desired **Transfers** option from list.

28. Click **Subcategories** box............ `Alt` + `S`

29. Select desired **Subcategories** option from list.

30. Click **Categories/Classes** .... `Alt` + `C`
    in **Customize** box.

31. Choose one of the following options:

- Categories .... `Alt` + `E`

- Classes .... `Alt` + `S`

Categories is the default above.

continu

Create Tax Summary Report (continued)

32. Click each category or class to include from **Select to Include** box.

For categories, the Select to Include box is a scroll box. If you have created more than seven classes, the Select to Include box also becomes a scroll box.

OR

Click  .... Alt + M

> *NOTE:* If one or more categories or classes are selected which you wish to deselect, click them in the **Select to Include** scroll box.

33. Click **Matching** .... Alt + G
    in **Customize** box.

Matching allows you to filter transactions appearing in reports based on a specific characteristic of a payee, category, class, memo or security.

34. Click **Payee Contains** .... Alt + P
     box.

35. Type payee name... *name*
    in dialog box.

    OR

    Select payee from box.

36. Click **Category Contains**...................... Alt + E

continued...

Create Tax Summary Report (continued)

37. Type category name .... *name*
    in dialog box.

    OR

    Select category from box.

38. Click **Class Contains** box..................... `Alt` + `S`

39. Type class name .... *name*
    in dialog box.

    OR

    Select class from box.

40. Press **Tab** .... `Tab`

41. Type memo.. *data*
    in **Memo Contains** dialog box.

42. Click [✔ OK] .... `↵`

TRANSACTION GROUPS

Groups recurring transactions you pay or add to your account at the same time.

Create Transaction Group

> *CAUTION:* Be sure all transactions included in the transaction group have been memorized. (See **MEMORIZE TRANSACTIONS**, page 169.)

1. Press **Ctrl+J** .... `Ctrl` + `J`

   OR

   a. Click **Lists** .... `Alt` + `L`

   b. Click **Scheduled Transaction**.................. `H`

2. Click ✚ **New** .... `Alt` +. `N`

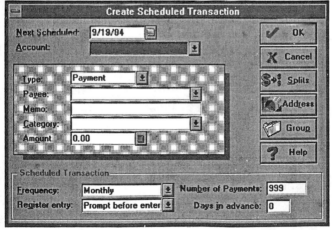

3. Click 📁 **Group** .... `Alt` + `G`

continued...

Create Transaction Group (continued)

4. Enter **Next** payment date .... *date*
   in date box.

5. Press **Tab** .... `Tab`

6. Select desired account from **Account** list.

7. Press **Tab** .... `Tab`

   If group contains noninvestment transactions:

   Click **Regular** .... `Alt` + `G`

   If group contains investment transactions:

   Click **Investment** .... `Alt` + `V`

8. Press **Tab** .... `Tab`

9. Type transaction **Group Name** .... *name*

10. Press **Tab** .... `Tab`

11. Select **Frequency** of payment from list.

12. Press **Tab** .... `Tab`

13. Enter **Number of Payments** .... *number*

14. Press **Tab** .... `Tab`

15. Select method of entering in register from **Register entry** list.

16. Press **Tab** .... `Tab`

17. Enter **Days in Advance** .... *number*

18. Click [✔ **OK**] .... `↵`

continue

Create Transaction Group (continued)

19. Highlight first transaction to assign to group.

20. Click ✔ Mark .... `Alt` + `M`

21. Repeat steps 19 and 20 for each transaction to assign to group.

22. Click 📥 Done .... `Alt` + `D`

Execute Transaction Group

1. Press **Ctrl+J** .... `Ctrl` + `J`

   OR

   a. Click **Lists** .... `Alt` + `L`

   b. Click **Scheduled Transaction**.................... `H`

2. Double-click transaction group you want to execute.

   OR

   a. Highlight transaction group you want to execute.

   b. Click 🏧 Pay .... `Alt` + `Y`

3. Enter transaction date .... *date*
   in **Record Scheduled Transaction** window.

   If a date is scheduled for the group, it appears in the Transaction Date field.

4. Click 🏧 Record .... `Alt` + `E`

Add Transaction to Transaction Group

> *CAUTION: Make sure the transaction you want to add has been memorized.*

1. Press **Ctrl+J** .... `Ctrl` + `J`

   OR

   a. Click **Lists** .... `Alt` + `L`

   b. Click **Scheduled Transaction** .... `H`

2. Highlight group to which you will add transaction.

3. Click `🔧 Edit` .... `Alt` + `I`

4. Highlight transaction you want to include in **Assign Transactions to Group** window.

5. Click `✔ Mark` .... `Alt` + `M`

7. Repeat steps **4-5** for each transaction you want to add to transaction group.

8. Click `➡️ Done` .... `Alt` + `D`

TRANSACTION REPORT

Create Transaction Report

1. Click

2. Click **Oth<u>e</u>r** .... Alt + E

3. Click **Transaction** .... Tab + ↓ ↑

4. Click **Customize** .... Alt + C

5. Select desired report dates from **Report Dates** list.

   OR

   a. Click **<u>f</u>rom** box .... Alt + F
      and enter date.

   b. Click **t<u>o</u>** box.................................... Alt + O
      and enter date.

   *NOTE: At the **<u>f</u>rom** and **t<u>o</u>** boxes, you can also
   access the drop-down calendar from which
   you can select starting and ending dates.*

6. Click **T<u>i</u>tle** box .... Alt + I

7. Type report title .... *title*

8. Click **S<u>u</u>btotal By** box............................ Alt + U

9. Select desired **S<u>u</u>btotal By** option from list.

10. Click **Sort <u>B</u>y** box.............................. Alt + B

11. Select desired **Sort <u>B</u>y** option from list.

continued...

Create Transaction Report (continued)

12. Click **Organization** box .... `Alt` + `Z`
13. Choose one of the following **Organization** options:
    - Income & expense
    - Cash flow basis

    If you want amounts rounded to nearest dollar:

    Deselect **Show Cents in Amounts** .... `Alt` + `S`

    If you do not want amounts rounded to nearest dollar:

    Select **Show Cents in Amounts** .... `Alt` + `S`

    If you want report to contain only totals:

    Select **Totals Only** .... `Alt` + `Y`

    If you want report to contain memo:

    Select **Memo** .... `Alt` + `M`

    If you do not want report to contain memo:

    Deselect **Memo** .... `Alt` + `M`

    If you want report to show category:

    Select **Category** .... `Alt` + `E`

    If you do not want report to show category:

    Deselect **Category** .... `Alt` + `E`

continu

Create Transaction Report (continued)

If you want report to show split transaction detail:

Select **Sp<u>l</u>it Transaction Detail**............ `Alt` + `P`

14. Click **<u>A</u>ccounts** .... `Alt` + `A`
    in **Customize** box.

15. Select each account to include in report from
    Accounts Used box.

    OR

    Click [🐎 **<u>M</u>ark All**] .... `Alt` + `M`

    OR

    Choose one of the following **Accounts Used**
    buttons to select all accounts in that category:

    - [🏛 **<u>B</u>ank**] .... `Alt` + `B`

    - [💵 **Cas<u>h</u>**] .... `Alt` + `H`

    - [💳 **Cre<u>d</u>it Card**] .... `Alt` + `D`

    - [📈 **<u>I</u>nvestment**] .... `Alt` + `I`

    - [🏠 **A<u>s</u>set**] .... `Alt` + `S`

    - [🚗 **Liabilit<u>y</u>**] .... `Alt` + `Y`

    *NOTE: If one or more accounts are selected which
             you wish to deselect, click them in the
             Accounts Used box.*

continued...

Create Transaction Report (continued)

16. Click **Transactions**............................... `Alt` + `N` in **Customize** box.

17. Click **Amounts** box............................. `Alt` + `M`

18. Choose one of the following **Amounts** options:

    - **All**

      Go to step 21.

    - **less than**

    - **equal to**

    - **greater than**

19. Click blank box to right of **Amounts** box.

20. Enter desired amount .... *number* relative to option you chose in step 18.

    NOTE: *For example, if you want the report to display only transactions of less than fifty dollars, you would choose* **less than** *in step 18, and type* 50 *in step 20.*

21. Choose one or more of the following options, if desired:

    - Include **U**nrealized Gains............... `Alt` + `U`

    - Ta**x**-related Transactions Only....... `Alt` + `X`

22. Click **Transaction Types** .... `Alt` + `T`

contin▶

Create Transaction Report (continued)

23. Select desired transaction type to appear from list.

24. Choose one or more of the following status options, if desired:

- <u>B</u>lank.. `Alt` + `B`

- Ne<u>w</u>ly Cleared .... `Alt` + `W`

- R<u>e</u>conciled .... `Alt` + `E`

Default values for the above options are preselected.

> NOTE: *To deselect any of the above options, click them.*

25. Click **Show <u>R</u>ows**............................... `Alt` + `R`
    in **Customize** box.

26. Click **<u>T</u>ransfers** box .... `Alt` + `T`

27. Select desired **<u>T</u>ransfers** option from list.

28. Click **<u>S</u>ubcategories** box .... `Alt` + `S`

29. Select desired **<u>S</u>ubcategories** option from list.

30. Click **<u>C</u>ategories/Classes**..................... `Alt` + `C`
    in **Customize** box.

31. Choose one of the following options:

- Cat<u>e</u>gories................................... `Alt` + `E`

- Cla<u>s</u>ses .... `Alt` + `S`

Categories is the default above.

continued...

Create Transaction Report (continued)

32. Click each category or class to include from **Select to Include** box.

For categories, the Select to Include box is a scroll box. If you have created more than seven classes, the Select to Include box also becomes a scroll box.

OR

Click ▓▓ **Mark All** .... Alt + M

> *NOTE:* *If one or more categories or classes are selected which you wish to deselect, click them in the Select to Include scroll box.*

33. Click **Matching** .... Alt + G
    in **Customize** box.

Matching allows you to filter transactions appearing in reports based on a specific characteristic of a payee, category, class, memo or security.

34. Click **Payee Contains** .... Alt + P
    box.

35. Type payee name .... *name*
    in dialog box.

    OR

    Select payee from box.

36. Click **Category Contains** .... Alt + E
    box.

37. Type category name .... *name*
    in dialog box.

    OR

continu

Create Transaction Report (continued)

Select category from box.

38. Click **Cla̲s̲s Contains** box .... Alt + S

39. Type class name... *name*
in dialog box.

    OR

    Select class from box.

40. Press **Tab** .... Tab

41. Type memo .... *data*
in **M̲emo Contains** dialog box.

42. Click ✔ **OK** .... Enter

UPDATE ACCOUNT BALANCES

Updates balances in other asset, liability and cash accounts.

1. Click

The Account List appears.

2. Double-click account you want to update (other
asset, liability or cash).

3. Click **Acti̲vities** .... Alt + V

4. Click **U̲pdate Balances** .... U

5. Click **Update C̲ash Balance** C

6. Enter **U̲pdate this account's balance to** .... *number*

continued...

282

7. Press **Tab** .... `Tab`

8. Type **Category for Adjustment** .... *category*

   NOTE: The above step is optional.

9. Press **Tab** .... `Tab`

10. Enter **Adjustment Date** .... *date*

11. Click [✔ **OK**] .... `⏎`

VOID CHECK OR DEPOSIT

Voids a transaction in the account register without deleting a record of it.

1. Click [Accts]

The Account List appears.

2. Double-click account containing transaction you want to void.

3. Highlight check or deposit you want to void.

4. Press **Ctrl+V** (**V**oid) .... `Ctrl` + `V`

   OR

   a. Click **Edit** .... `Alt` + `E`

   b. Click **Void Transaction** .... `V`

5 Click [**Record**] .... `Alt` + `C`

WRITE CHECKS

Fill Out Check

—FROM ACCOUNTS LIST WINDOW—

1. Double-click account from which you want to write checks.

2. Press **Ctrl+W** (**W**rite Checks) .... Ctrl + W

   OR

   a. Click **Acti_v_ities** .... Alt + V

   b. Click **Write Checks** .... W

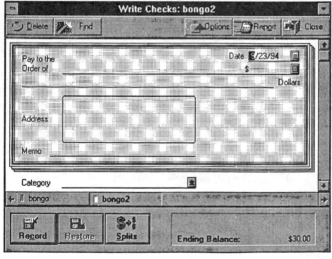

3. Enter date .... *date* you want on check.

4. Press **Tab** .... Tab

continued...

284

Fill Out Check (continued)

5. Type payee name .... *name*

    To select payee from list:

    a. Click down arrow .... ⊞

    b. Select desired payee.

6. Press **Tab** .... Tab

7. Enter payment amount .... *amount*

8. Press **Tab** .... Tab

Quicken writes out the amount on the next line.

9. Type payee name and address...*name* and *address*
    if you are mailing check
    in an Intuit window envelope.

    NOTE: The above step is optional.

10. Press **Tab** .... Tab
    until the memo field
    is reached.

11. Type memo.. *data*

    NOTE: The above step is optional.

12. Press **Tab** .... Tab

13. Type category or class .... *category* or *class*

    To select from list:

    a. Click down arrow .... ⊞

    b. Highlight category or class.

continue➜

c. Press **Tab** .... `Tab`

NOTE: The above step is optional.

14. Click ▣ **Record** .... `Alt` + `C`

15. Click ▣ **Close**

Edit Check

1. Click ▣ Accts

The Account List appears.

2. Double-click account from which you want to edit check.

3. Click ▣ Check .... `Ctrl` + `W`

    OR

    a. Click **Acti̲vities** .... `Alt` + `V`

    b. Click **W̲rite Checks** .... `W`

    To locate check to edit:

continued...

Fill Out Check (continued)

Press **PgUp**, **PgDn** .... `Page Up` `Page Down`
to scroll through checks.

OR

a. Click `Find` .... `Alt` + `I`
and enter search information.
(See FIND, page 91.)

b. Click `>> Find` .... `Alt` + `N`

4. Make necessary changes.

5. Click `Record` .... `Alt` + `C`

Delete Check

—FROM ACCOUNTS WINDOW—

1. Double-click account from which you want to edit
check.

2. Click `Check` .... `Ctrl` + `W`

OR

a. Click **Activities** .... `Alt` + `V`

b. Click **Write Checks** .... `W`

To locate check to delete:

continue

Delete Check (continued)

Press **PgUp/PgDn**................................ `Page Up` `Page Down`
to scroll through checks.

OR

a. Click [Find] .... `Alt` + `I`
and enter search information.
(See **FIND**, page 91.)

b. Click [>> Find] .... `Alt` + `N`

—*WHEN YOU LOCATE CHECK*—

3. Press [🚫 Delete] .... `Ctrl` + `D`

4. Click [✔ OK] .... `⏎`

YEAR-END ACTIVITIES

Copy Prior Year Transactions to Another File and Keep Current File Intact

1. Click **File** .... `Alt` + `F`

2. Click **Year-End Copy** .... `Y`

3. Click **Archive** .... `Alt` + `A`

4. Click [✔ OK] .... `Enter`

5. Make necessary changes to filename, archive file location and archive transaction date.

continued...

Copy Prior Year Transactions to Another File and Keep Current File Intact (continued)

6. Click [✔ OK] .... [↵]

   To use current file:

   Click **U̲se Current File** .... [Alt] + [U]

   To use archive file:

   Click **U̲se Archive File** .... [Alt] + [S]

7. Click [✔ OK] .... [Enter]

Copy Prior Year Transactions to Another File and Clear Current File

1. Click **F̲ile** .... [Alt] + [F]

2. Click **Y̲ear-End Copy** .... [Y]

3. Click **S̲tart New Year** .... [Alt] + [S]

4. Click [✔ OK] .... [Enter]

5. Type filename .... *filename*

6. Press **Tab** .... [Tab]

7. Type date .... *date*
   you want to delete transactions
   older than, from current file.

continu

Copy Prior Year Transactions to Another File and Clear Current File (continued)

8. Press **Tab** .... `Tab`

   If desired location is different from default location:

   Type current file location .... *location*

9. Click ✔ **OK** .... `↵`

10. Select desired option:

    - Use old file

    - Use file for new year.

11. Click ✔ **OK** .... `↵`

APPENDIX

QUICK KEYS AND SHORTCUTS

FILE OPERATIONS

`Ctrl` + `B`   Back up file

`Ctrl` + `O`   Open file

HELP KEY

`F1`   Gives you help with the current window or menu.

INVESTMENTS

`Ctrl` + `U`   Goes to Portfolio view.

`-` or `+`   Decreases/increases price by 1/8.

`Ctrl` + `Y`   Security, select or set up

REGISTER AND WRITE CHECKS

`Ctrl` + `A`	Account, select or set up.
`Ctrl` + `C`	Category and Transfer, select up/down.
`Ctrl` + `L`	Class, select up/down.
`Ctrl` + `Ins`	Copies field in register.
`Shift` + `Ins`	Pastes field in register.
`Ctrl` + `D`	Deletes transaction or split line.
`Ctrl` + `F`	Finds transaction.
`Ctrl` + `N`	Goes to new transaction.
`Ctrl` + `J`	Groups transactions, set up/recall.
`Ctrl` + `I`	inserts transaction or splits line
`Ctrl` + `M`	Memorizes transaction.
`Ctrl` + `P`	Prints.
`Ctrl` + `T`	Recalls memorized transaction.
Type payee name	QuickFill automatically recalls transaction.
`Tab`	QuickFill automatically completes transaction.
`Ctrl` + `↑` `↓`	QuickFill list, scroll up/down.
`↵` `Ctrl` + `↵`	Records transaction.
`Ctrl` + `S`	Splits transaction.
`Ctrl` + `X`	Transfers, go to.
`Ctrl` + `C`	Transfers, select account for.

MOVE IN WINDOW

`Tab` / `Shift` + `Tab`	Next/Previous field or column
`Home`	Beginning of field
`Home` , `Home`	First field in transaction or window, or first report row
`Home` , `Home` , `Home`	First transaction in window
`Home` , `Home` , `Home` , `Home`	First transaction in register
`Ctrl` + `Home`	First transaction, or upper left corner of report
`End`	End of field
`End` , `End`	Last field in transaction or window, or last report row
`End` , `End` , `End`	Last transaction in window
`End` , `End` , `End` , `End`	Last transaction in register
`Ctrl` + `End`	Last transaction, or lower right corner of report
`Page Down` / `Page Up`	Next/previous window or check
`Ctrl` + `Page Down`	Next month
`Ctrl` + `Page Up`	Previous month
`↑` / `↓`	Up/down one row

SPECIAL KEYS

`-`	Decreases date or check number.
`+`	Increases date or check number.
`Ctrl` + `R`	Goes to register.
`Ctrl` + `W`	Goes to **Write Checks**.
`Ctrl` + `K`	Goes to **Financial Calendar**.
`Ctrl` + `H`	Goes to **View Loans**.
`Ctrl` + `U`	Goes to **Portfolio View**.
`Ctrl` + `Z`	QuickZoom report amount.
First letter of item	Selects item in drop-down list.

DATES

`T`	Today
`M`	First day of this month
`H`	Last day of this month
`Y`	First day of this year
`R`	Last day of this year

GLOSSARY

NOTE: *For a more comprehensive financial glossary, see the **Help Glossary** in Quicken 4 for Windows.*

Amortization 1: An accounting method by which the cost of an asset is spread out over its life.

2: The liquidation of a long-term debt by means of regular installment payments.

Annuity Insurance in which the insured pays a predetermined sum to a life insurance company so that, at a predetermined time, s/he receives a sum of money for a specific period or for life.

Asset Any property having monetary value.

BillMinder A Quicken feature reminding you to pay your bills.

Bond A long-term obligation of a government or corporation, where the bond issuer promises to pay a specific amount of interest over a period of time and repay the principal on the date of maturity.

Budget Helps you plan your income and expenses and then compares your actual income and expenses to your plan.

Buttons Graphics representing Quicken 3 for Windows commands.

Category Labels you can apply to transactions to track how much you are spending on particular items. *(See Class, below.)*

CheckFree Quicken's electronic bill paying method. This service is offered by the CheckFree Corporation of Columbus, Ohio.

Check A promissory note used to pay debts. The note is counted against money held in a bank account, and is paid automatically by the bank, provided there is enough money in the account to cover the check.

Class Labels you can apply to transactions to track how much you are spending on particular items; more detailed than categories *(see above)*.

Clipboard Area of Quicken where copied information is held until it is transferred to another document.

GLOSSARY (continued)

Copying Reproducing data from one location to another.

Debt Cash, goods or services owed by one person to another.

Default Settings automatically used by the program that can be modified.

Dividend The portion of a corporation's earnings distributed to its stockholders, according to the number and kind of stock they own.

Editing Changing account contents.

Equity
1: An investment representing an ownership interest.
2: The difference between the amount a property can be sold for and the claims held against it.
3: The excess of assets over liabilities.

Escrow The placement of assets with a third party to ensure the performance of the terms of a contract.

Expense Anything you spend money on.

Field Area within a window where you can enter specific information.

File A collection of Quicken accounts and information.

File name The name given to a collection of Quicken accounts and information.

Financial calendar A Quicken feature that helps you to keep track of anticipated transactions.

Font Style and size of character typeface. Used to change the appearance of printed checks and reports.

Graph A visual interpretation of data in the form of a bar, line or pie chart.

Ginnie Mae Popular name for **Government National Mortgage Association** (also **GNMA**), a U.S. government corporation guaranteeing timely payment of interest and principal on securities backed by Federal Housing Administration-insured and Veterans' Administration guaranteed mortgages.

Gross income Income from all sources during a given accounting period.

Gross profit   The revenues from sales of goods or services minus the cost of the goods or services sold, but not deducting overhead or other expenses.

Icon   Graphics representing Quicken 3 for Windows commands found on the iconbar.

Income   *(See **Gross income**, above.)*

Investment   Money put into a business, stocks, bonds, real estate or anything, for the purpose of obtaining an income and/or profit.

IRA   Abbreviation for **Individual Retirement Account**, a tax-sheltered investment plan permitting a person to accumulate funds for retirement by making tax-deferred contributions to the account.

Keogh   A retirement savings plan for the self-employed. The maximum one can contribute annually is set by law and is fully tax-deductible until it is withdrawn.

Liability   Any debt giving a creditor a claim on the borrower's assets.

Liquid Asset   Any property that is cash, or is readily converted into cash.

Loan value   The maximum amount a lender can loan against collateral.

Margin trading   Buying securities using a broker's credit to pay for part of them.

Menu   A list of commands, grouped by subject.

Modem   An electronic device that attaches to your computer and allows you to transmit information via the telephone system to other computers.

Mortgage   A long-term loan for land and/or buildings (real property) in which the property serves as security for the loan.

Mutual Fund   An investment company that buys and sells its own shares and invests its capital in the securities of other companies or other enterprises.

Net assets   *(See **Net worth**, below.)*

Net income   The difference between a company's or individual's income and its costs and expenses over a period of time.

GLOSSARY (continued)

Net worth   All assets minus all liabilities of an individual or business. Same as **net assets**.

Obligation   Any form of debt, such as a bond, note, bill or IOU.

Panic   A wave of fear in the financial community that the economy is going into a steep decline. This brings on a period of frantic selling of securities and commodities in hopes of beating all-time low prices. The selling itself, however, can bring on the economic decline that was feared.

Pension plan   An investment in which regular contributions over time are invested, with earnings tax-deferred and reinvested, and which is paid out as a series of regular payments after retirement.

Profit   Any excess of income over cost of obtaining it.

Qcards   On-screen messages displayed by Quicken to help you enter the correct information.

QuickFill   Quicken's shortcut feature that automatically memorizes transaction details the first time you enter them. In the future, as you begin to type in the same information, Quicken recognizes the transaction and automatically fills In the details for you. If the details are incorrect, simply type the new information over the QuickFill data.

Reconcile   Brings your Quicken records into balance with your bank records.

Record   Stores the information you have entered in a transaction and updates all balances automatically.

Register   A window for each account on which you enter information about that account. You can see an overview of activity for an account by looking at its register.

Report   Allows you to view detailed information about your accounts, and the activity taking place in those accounts.

298

Restore
1: A button in the register that you can click to correct a mistake made while entering a transaction. The transaction reverts to the way it was before you started to enter information.
2: The act of using back-up files to replace Quicken files that have been damaged or lost.

Risk The possibility of financial loss.

Savings Bank A financial institution, generally state-chartered, and usually organized as a mutual association, as opposed to a corporation.

Scroll A vertical or horizontal cursor movement displaying portions of the window existing beyond the limits of the screen.

Security A written instrument that shows equity, rights to equity or debt in a corporation, government or other enterprise.

Share The smallest unit of stock offered by a corporation.

Split transaction A Quicken transaction categorized with multiple categories or classes. Allows for very specific tracking of spending and earning.

Stock A share in the ownership of a corporation, representing a claim on its earnings and assets.

Tax-shelter An investment where one earns a return but postpones or avoids making income tax payments within the limit of tax-law.

Transfer Sending money from one Quicken account to another.

Tutorials Quicken files explaining how to use Windows and Quicken.

Yield The rate of return on an investment, expressed as a percentage.